Alexander Anderson

The Two Angels

And Other Poems

Alexander Anderson

The Two Angels
And Other Poems

ISBN/EAN: 9783744711135

Printed in Europe, USA, Canada, Australia, Japan

Cover: Foto ©Thomas Meinert / pixelio.de

More available books at **www.hansebooks.com**

POEMS.

THE TWO ANGELS

AND

OTHER POEMS.

BY

ALEXANDER ANDERSON,

Author of "A Song of Labour, and other Poems,"

KIRKCONNEL, DUMFRIES-SHIRE.

WITH AN INTRODUCTORY SKETCH BY

REV. GEORGE GILFILLAN,

DUNDEE,

Author of "The Bards of the Bible," &c., &c.

LONDON: SIMPKIN, MARSHALL, & CO.
EDINBURGH AND GLASGOW: JOHN MENZIES & CO.

1875.

INTRODUCTORY SKETCH.

The appearance of a new volume of Poems from the pen of Mr Alexander Anderson, of Kirkconnel, so widely known by the *nom-de-plume* of "Surfaceman," seems to justify a short sketch of his life, and an appraisement of his poetry. This account shall at least have the two merits of Sincerity and of Shortness. And first, of the events of his life. Mr Anderson was born on the 30th of April 1845, at Kirkconnel, a small village at the upper end of Dumfriesshire; his boyhood was spent at Crocketford, another small village in the lower end of Galloway. At a humble school he gained the rudiments of his early education. Here, he tells us himself, he was not remarkable for any particular cleverness or aptitude for learning. He was a good penman, however, took great delight in acquiring what Dominie Sampson calls "a firm, current, clear, and legible hand," and became a caligrapher. The notanda about himself, which he has kindly sent us, and his correspondence, prove that he can write in both senses of the term—not scrawl inscrutabilities, as too many of his kindred are in the habit of doing. He was a good sketcher, too, and enjoyed a local fame for colouring. He became the member of an improvised Academy of Youths, every one of whom was bound to provide, at short stated periods, a sketch, or rather daub, to be criticised by the rest. The result was neither pleasant nor profitable, for he tells us "that our strictures were often of the most pungent kind, and violent disputes, that would last for days, were the invariable results of our love for Art." " Deep in colour, they were deficient in harmony." "Surfaceman" says—" I can still see myself trudging to school, satchel on back, and stopping now and then to see if my masterpiece was receiving any damage in its transit."

From these beginnings a great painter—a Harvey or a Wilkie— might have been looked for, but he soon turned from colours to word-painting, and, like other juvenile bards,

"Lisped in numbers, for the numbers came."

And the first thing that struck his young eye was the common and even ludicrous incident of a man being hit by a snowball. There are elements in this very capable of treatment. The pompous strut of the venerable magistrate or divine who is the victim, striving to maintain his usual dignity while dipping his feet heavily into the thick slush—or three-foot snow—the look of surprise, blended with rage and confusion, with which he feels the sudden ball lighting on the nape of his neck and deranging the grand repose of his white choker, and turns round for vengeance— and the shy, timid, yet gleesome glance of the urchin, as he, with reverted head and hand still extended, speeds away like lightning across the street, while roars of young laughter attest the triumph felt at the abasement of the Rev. Pompous Turkeycock, and drown his fierce ejaculations of fury, which sound like half-formed and frost-bit *oaths* in the distance. We would liked to have seen " Surfaceman's" handling of such a scene, and regret that, though much applauded by his companions, his poem has not been preserved by himself. He indulged at this period in doggerel rhymes; every sentiment that he deemed worth recording he put into verse, and he blames this for the stiff prose which he says he writes now, as if head and hand, so early accustomed to rhyming, disdained to descend to vulgar prose. He quotes Shenstone to shelter himself, who says somewhere "that Pegasus must not be yoked with a dray horse."

On the other hand, there are others of a poetical temperament who regret that they did not in early youth learn to rhyme and write verse with as much facility as to indite prose, and who think that by this their prose would have been improved, and any poetical attempt would have cost them less mechanical labour, and allowed them more freedom and ease in the act of composition.

"Surfaceman," after writing a number of Satires, Epistles, and other Poems, submitted them all to a fiery baptism not long ago. He should, as did Pope or Thomson, we forget which, have first written an account of their various demerits, and suspended it like an ancient *scroll* of heresy around their necks! There is no doubt a savage luxury in such cremations, but we doubt on the whole their wisdom. Early productions, if not proofs of power, are marks of progress. As such they should be preserved. Even as to the question of pleasure, we are mistaken if to burn boyish poetry or prose gives such a thrilling tingling joy as to find after long years specimens of them which had gone astray, and be thus, as Foster has it, enabled to "resume the departed state of our souls." "Surfaceman" seems to have burned his productions when, we will suppose, he was about 25; had he waited till he was 50, or older, he would have been delighted had they been still extant. And we have no doubt many of them would be excellent in themselves, as well as interesting from memory and associations.

He returned with his parents from Crocketford to his native village, and, coinciding with this in time, was his entire abandonment for a season of poetry. One reason was his growing conviction of the worthlessness of what he had written; and he adds very naively, as another, that the nature of his employment (working in a quarry) was probably not conducive to that kind of study.

He now began to extend his reading, but at first in a wrong direction. He revelled in what he calls "claptrap," by which we understand sensational literature—novels, plays, &c.—which, not to injure a reader, requires on his part a strong youthful appetite and digestion. The healthy boy, at a certain time of life, and who enjoys plenty of exercise, may be permitted to eat any amount of hips, haws, brambles, sloes, and will do so with impunity. And so with a strong-minded, intellectual boy. It little matters at a certain period what such a person reads. The boy will read, the youth will study, and the man will think and act. But he will not long, if of the right stamp, remain satisfied with such food, and will begin to hunger for better books. While devouring trash Mr Anderson's love and practice of poetry were kept in entire abeyance. The fountain of song was sealed, and slumbered under Circulating Library mud mountains, till at last "Strong Death" removed the incubus. A beloved brother, not older than 26, was taken away, and "To One in Eternity" was the result. Thus the spring was opened, and has never since been shut. Along with a love of poetry re-awakened, there arose in his mind a desire for studying languages. He began with French, procured a grammar, became his own master, and, by dint of persevering, and utilizing every spare moment, cut out a royal road to learning; and after mastering French therewith, carried it on to the more difficult regions of German and Italian, and says proudly yet modestly, "Now I can appreciate in my own way in their own tongue the mighty voices of Goethe, Schiller, and Dante." Which among these great Spirits would not have been ready to cry, "This is true fame," had they known that their masterpieces—Werter, the Faust, the Robbers, and the Divina Comedia—were read and appreciated at the bottom of a Dumfriesshire quarry? "Surfaceman" grants that his knowledge of these authors was and is yet imperfect; but says that it is a great pleasure to him, and it must be a source of genuine inspiration.

His connection with the *People's Friend*—a journal which has occupied well a field which has been long unoccupied in Scotland, since, at least, the days of "Hogg's Instructor," and been an outlet to the overflowing young intellect and genius of our country, particularly amongst the uneducated but aspiring classes—began in 1870. Previous to this he had written a copy of verses in the *People's Journal* on Mr Ferguson's famous but now forgotten and forgiven escapade against Robert Burns. The first poem in the *Friend* was a poem on John Keats, which may be found third in his first volume of poems.* After this he became a regular contributor, and was very highly appreciated by its readers, till at last, in the autumn of 1873, he was encouraged to publish his "Song of Labour and other Poems"—a book which met an instant and most generous reception both from the press and the public. Of it we wrote at the time—"Here is verily a Sign of the Times—a perfect

---

* The poem referred to—the only one reprinted from the former volume—will be found at page 211.

phenomenon—a volume of true poetry, testifying to a powerful, and, more wonderful still, a well-cultivated mind, by a working railway navvy or surfaceman on the Glasgow and South-Western Railway. The Ayrshire Ploughman, the Edinburgh Barber, the Paisley Weaver, the Glasgow Pattern-drawer, the Clydesdale Miner, the Aberdeen Policeman are scarcely so wonderful as the Kirkconnel Surfaceman."

A surfaceman Mr Anderson still contentedly continues, residing with his parents in the humble village of Kirkconnel, and unmarried. He has his favourite books, pen, ink, and paper, to amuse him in the evenings, and friends, too, who drop in now and then to have a quiet chat. He adds, " What more have I to wish for ? I have the great rush and whirl of the world going past me in trains through the day when at my work, and at night the cool healthy calm of my native village." We believe a purer and simpler-minded man does not exist. He sends on his passions rushing with the trains—he retains in his own bosom and home the peace which passeth all understanding.

The volume he now presents to the world is distinguished by great variety of subject and of modes of treatment. It has a number of sweet Scottish verses, plaintive or pawky, such as " Jenny wi' the Airn Teeth," " Cuddle Doon," and " Jamie's Wee Chair." It has some strains of a higher mood, reminding us of Keats in their rich imagination, such as " Alexis" and the "Two Angels." He has some poems written in what may be called peculiarly his own style—a style befitting his trade, a style of iron and fire—such as " Blood on the Wheel," " The Poet," and " By the Grave of Livingstone." All these are excellent in different ways. But the highest effort, if not also the most decided success, is his series of sonnets, entitled, " In Rome." And certainly this is a remarkable series. The mere fact of a young " Surfaceman" grappling with a subject which has employed and tasked such pens as that of Byron's, Madame De Stael's, and Goethe's, to name only a few, and not failed, is itself very high praise. We will not say that " Surfaceman" has entirely succeeded in an attempt at which angels might " bashful look," to pourtray the ruins of Rome—rich enough when Dyer wrote about them a hundred years ago, but ineffably enriched since by the dust of Shelley and of Keats, and by the deeds of Garibaldi, not to speak of the magic light which Childe Harold has cast upon it as from an unsetting Italian sunset, in the glorious Fourth Canto of his " Pilgrimage." Still, " In Rome" is a production of great genius, and is precisely best on those points of interest which have lately been added to the Eternal City. "Surfaceman" does not shine in the "Colosseum," or the "Laocöon," or the " Dying Gladiator." We think he had better have left these alone. But when he speaks of Shelley, and especially of Keats, he speaks like a true poet, and appropriately tells us that the best thing he has brought from Rome is

" A wither'd violet from Keats's grave."

G. G.

DUNDEE, September, 1875.

CONTENTS.

	Page
Agnes Died,	19
Alexis,	37
A' His Lane,	203
A Song for my Fellows,	74
A Song of Progress,	51
A Walk to Pamphy Linns,	103
Behind Time,	100
Blood on the Wheel,	58
By the Grave of Livingstone,	55
Chateaux en Espagne,	27
City and Village,	170
Cockie-roosie-ride,	174
Cuddle Doon,	72
Daft Ailie,	197
/ David Gray,	151
Dingle Doozie,	146
Early Poet Life,	69
God Wrapt Him,	226
Granny Grey Pow,	176
In Kirkconnel Old Churchyard,	154
/ In Rome—a Poem in Sonnets,	121
Is Wee Jamie Wauken Yet?	148
In Tempe,	32
In the Vanguard,	81
Jamie's Wee Chair,	67
Jenny wi' the Airn Teeth,	61
Jim's Whistle,	215
/ John Keats,	211
Ledgie Cooper,	77
Livingstone,	54

	Page
Look to the East,	208
Mary,	159
May Middleton's Tam,	193
Move Upward,	218
Oor First Wee Graves,	187
Over the Sea, Annie,	160
Rabelais,	140
Reading the Book,	149
Rid of his Engine,	207
Rock Him till He Grows a Mannie,	86
Song of the Engine,	221
The Bowgie Man,	161
The Cuckoo,	118
The Deil's Stane,	90
The Fiddler o' Boglebriggs,	178
The First-Foot,	96
The Last Sweet Walk,	143
The Lost Eden Found Again,	120
The New Year,	99
The Old School-House,	88
The Open Secret,	230
The Poet,	63
The Questioning Angels,	213
The San' Man,	205
The Singers,	225
The Two Angels,	9
The Veiled Memnon,	113
The Weary Weird,	163
The Worship of Sorrow,	65
To a City Friend,	189
To an Old Schoolfellow,	44
Two Eyes,	217
Where I am Lying Now,	85

THE TWO ANGELS.

POEMS.

THE TWO ANGELS.

TWO angels, as I grew up glad and gay
    From golden infancy,
Were with me, walking all along the way
    On either side of me.

The one at my right hand was sweet and fair,
    His brow spoke noble things,
As if God's breath had lain a moment there
    In blessings. His white wings

All radiantly rose above his head,
    Their shadow fell on me
Like sweet dews falling when the night is dead,
    The stars half out to see.

I walk'd within their shadow, fearing none,
    Nor had one dread of blame;
This angel and my spirit were as one,
    And all our thoughts the same.

My heart had golden music, which to hear
    Beating and singing on,
He sometimes stopp'd and downward leant his ear,
    Smiling to hear its tone.

All through my childhood with such dew besprent
    I walk'd, and watch'd his beck;
He still grew brighter, and as on we went,
    His arm lay round my neck.

I felt its pressure soft and sweet to feel,
    That ever closer grew
When, at his feet in twilight, I would kneel
    And lisp my prayers through.

What beauty and what splendour crown'd him then,
    What light within his eyes!
As if a flush of glory came again
    Fresh from his own sweet skies.

Thus on we went, and all along our way
    Cerulean-colour'd things
Rose up, and made a bountiful display
    Of all their forms and wings.

Yet all this while the angel at my left
    Kept pace with us, but he
Bent down his brow, which was of light bereft,
    And dread and black to see.

He, too, had splendour seraph-like and bright
    Wrapt as in some thin shroud,
And lurid as the sultry summer light
    Girding a thunder-cloud.

He strode a pace behind, and all the while
    A triumph ill conceal'd
Lay on his brow, and mingling with his smile
    A strange, dread fear did yield.

And ever as we went, behind there came
    Strange whispers from his wings,
That stirr'd me, touching like a secret flame
    That leaps and keenly stings.

And as I felt this probeless change within
    I turn'd in mute distress
To my right guide, but something did begin
    To make his beauty less.

His brow grew clouded; paler light began
    To stretch along his robe;
A duller light lay on his wings' wide span,
    And thereat I did sob,

Weeping, not knowing what to think, for all
    His glory still grew dim,
Paling, like leaves that in the winter fall,
    And pass'd away to him,

The angel at my left, who, with a smile
    Of hate and secret pride
Came, as if bent on working some great guile,
    With one leap to my side.

He took my hand, which, at the touch of his,
    Shook as in deep annoy,
Still whispering in strange unusual bliss—
    "Life is before: enjoy."

I turn'd from that strange whisper to the right,
    And he who watch'd me there
Took for a moment all his former light,
    And, smiling wondrous fair,

His clasp grew firmer round my neck, as still
    In deep, sweet tones, he said—
"Heed not the angel on thy left, for ill
    He follows up thy tread.

He proffers thee the richest wines to cool
    Thy lusting lips, and sends
Thy passions, like wild things grown out of rule
    To all ignoble ends.

Each fruit, rich melting in thy mouth, shall fill
    Thy eager breathing soul
With dreams of other pathways for thy will,
    And purposes shall roll

Within thee, many-sided, that shall make
    Insatiable delight,
Still pointing to fair paths which thou shalt take
    With panting zeal and might.

But in the end, when all these things have pass'd,
    He will fling up his trust
And leave thee, death's thin arms around thee cast,
    Thy heart chokefull of dust.

But heed thou well my counsel, for I come
    To guide thy feeble feet,
Leading thee upward to that far-off home
    Where rest is long and sweet."

THE TWO ANGELS.

So spake my guiding angel; little truth
    For my expanding breast
Had his sweet words; for I was touch'd with youth,
    And felt a wild unrest

Creeping through all my being, as the wind
    Creeps through the evening grass;
And new-found feelings were within my mind
    That would not act or pass

Into fruition, but were there alive,
    And sweetly would they speak
In happiest tones, that made sweet fancies strive,
    Till flush'd were brow and cheek.

Then through my heart delicious madness ran,
    Making it beat full strong;
And headlong into all the miraged plan
    I wildly rush'd along.

I steep'd myself in bubbling wells of sense,
    Nor felt my passion tire,
But widen'd out in the omnipotence
    Of young-fledged, sweet desire.

And I grew earthier, heeding not the guide
    Who still walk'd on the right;
But turn'd to him upon the left with pride
    That had a touch of spite.

For, blinded with my own all headlong aims,
    I held, in spite of him
My better angel, ways to countless shames
    That mist-like came to dim

My better being. I felt sudden pow'r
    Grow up within the breast
To act those thoughts that cropp'd up hour by hour,
    At the left angel's hest.

He, too, had now one seeming radiant arm
    Around me as in love;
Its touch had something of a wizard's charm,
    'Gainst which I never strove:

But led by it I went like one stone-blind,
    Guided by touch and will;
I had no sympathy with beast or kind,
    But my own pleasure still.

Then as I saw the angel on the right,
    Lo! with dejected pace
He walk'd, but now his form had lost its light
    And splendour; all his face

Was muffled up and hidden by the fold
    Of a dark veil, through which
No light came, or a feature to behold,
    Or even voice to teach.

A ghostliness was round him as he stepp'd,
    Chilling my inmost heart;
A momentary tearful sorrow crept
    Throughout me as a part

Of his good influence, not yet wholly dead,
    Though sunk and buried o'er
By dust from the left angel's evil tread,
    Now sounding more and more.

Then as if claiming mastery, he rose,
    And in wild whirls of might,
Strove to push back—as one might push his foes—
    The angel from the right.

But still he kept his place, all ghostly calm,
    And once he cried to me—
"Help thou thyself, and I will give thee balm
    To heal thy soul in thee."

I heard, and heeded not, but went my way
    Through landscapes of rich view;
While round the right-hand angel, day by day,
    The deep folds closer grew.

And now he guided not, but ever stood
    At my right hand, all dumb,
Like some dread ghost that hath a midnight mood
    For walking. He would come

At times, when I was half awake in dreams,
    Fair as my childhood saw,
And brighter than the full broad summer beams,
    And I would gaze in awe:

Till all the memory of that early look,
    My kneeling by his knee,
The gentle warning and the soft rebuke,
    Would waken up in me

A bitterness, and dim prophetic dread
    That through my heart would creep,
And, ceasing not, was with me though I hid
    Myself in senseless sleep.

Betimes when I would waken up, I felt
    Tears lying soft and sweet
Upon my cheek, as if in sleep I knelt
    By that good angel's feet,

Lisping, as in pure childhood, that sweet pray'r
    My heart had now forgot,
For other things that found a harbour there,
    And fed the downward thought.

Then I became a prey to questionings;
    Each mute thing had a voice,
Asking, "Dost thou, too, stand amid brave things,
    Yet makest such a choice?"

This question struck me, as a dart will strike,
    And turning round to see
The angel at my left, a deep dislike
    Rose up at once in me.

For, looking in his eyes, I saw dim flame
    Burning by fits within;
And on his brow there was a mark of shame—
    Background to lust and sin.

The lurid glory which before had pow'r
    To draw me on and on,
Lessen'd its light, and weaken'd hour by hour,
    Till he was left alone.

And lo! the garment hiding limb and chest
    Fell from him, and I saw
A serpent coil'd around his waist and breast,
    As if in act to draw

The red heart from its hiding-place. I shriek'd
  At that dread sight, and fell
Prone on my face, while utter madness wreak'd
  Within me a dread spell,

That lay upon me like a sudden weight,
  Pressing me deeper down,
Until I cried for help from this dread state,
  Like one about to drown.

Then suddenly a clasp was on my arm,
  I felt myself upraised;
While in my ear a whisper, "Fear no harm,"
  Was spoken. Half abased

I look'd up, and my better angel stood
  Beside me—a great light
Came through the thick folds of his veil, subdued
  Like moon's in summer night.

"Come thou with me, and I will gently guide,"
  This he spoke soft and low;
"Will ever stead thee, standing by thy side,
  Through earthly things below."

So taking heart I took his hand and went,
  Fear still upon my mind;
And still my face at times was backward bent
  On him who walk'd behind.

But as we went he still fell further back;
  His features ever grew
Deeper and darker, till they changed to black
  Of most intensest hue.

And lo! the serpent which was coil'd around
　His breast seem'd to have stung
His heart with venom through, until the wound
　A tainted odour flung

Upon the air, and onward swift and strong
　It came. I paled and shrunk
At its dread breath, until I fell among
　My fears again and sunk

Downward, my heart within me drinking fears,
　Like water from a cup,
Till the good angel whisper'd, "Dry thy tears,
　And raise thy vision up."

I turn'd, and looking upward, all his face
　Was radiant with a look
Of wide supernal joy, and I could trace
　The light I could not brook

For its keen splendour, to a cross above
　Whereon a Godlike One
Was stretch'd. His face was one great smile of love
　That could for all atone.

I saw, and knelt, and kneeling down with me
　The angel round my neck
Placed his soft arm, and whisper'd soothingly—
　" Make thyself free from speck :

For now all things will work for good, and now
　Thy heart shall be more pure ;
There shall be pow'r within thee, and a glow
　Making each footstep sure."

"Look thou behind." I look'd, and far away
  My evil angel stood,
And in his heart in knotted coilings lay
  The serpent's writhing brood.

"Look thou before." I look'd, and ere I wist
  He whom the cross had borne
In our own semblance, the most perfect Christ,
  Heeding nor hate nor scorn,

Walk'd, clearing pathways for my feet. He pass'd
  Through shadows dim and dark,
But still behind a glorious light He cast,
  To let me see my mark.

And so I follow, having little dread,
  Knowing when death is nigh
That right-hand angel will uplift my head,
  And kiss me ere I die.

AGNES DIED.

"A pure sweet life, that came upon our earth,
Stay'd for a space, and then went back to heaven."

I KNOW not how it is, but all the past
  Is with me, speaking of its early things,
And in its voice a clearer, sweeter chord
Is heard, and I, half in a waking dream,
Musing upon the music, think awhile
Like one who on a sudden sees two paths,
And halts uncertain which to take, until
One tells him, and he straightway goes his way;

AGNES DIED.

So, thinking on that voice, a gracious time
Comes back, and in its light I stand, and say,
A touch of sorrow in my whisper, "Strange
That there should be so much to move my soul
In words so plain and simple—*Agnes died.*"

But let me trace a pathway through the years,
Whose tombs are pillars that bear up the past,
And lay my hand upon that time when she
Knew not the shadow creeping on her cheek,
Dulling its roses, but in happy strength
Met the sweet brow of every day that brought
Glad youth and all its fairy world to her.
The first of our acquaintance sprung from where
Most human friendships spring—the school, and we,
Half shy and strange at first, broke up the ground
With words of little use to older heads,
And questions, such as owe their birth to all
The inventive gift of children free to choose
What their quick fancy thinks is best; and now
You may be looking for a long account
Of wandering home in summer afternoons;
Of holidays in which we tasted heaven;
Of the long looking forward to that time
When six weeks made us like the kings and queens
In now forgotten tales. But not for me
Is such a task; I lack the words, not thought;
For, looking back, the glory of that time
Rises like light upon the dark, and makes
A halo round it, beautiful and bright,
As if we saw the sun through our own tears.

So we grew up, and with the kindly years
Our friendship grew the stronger, and I watch'd

With a boy lover's eye the opening bud
Of her sweet spirit; saw its infant germ
Expand beneath the breathing of the years,
Touch the soft outline of her gentle form,
And tint the cheek with colour like the rose
When first it breaks its little cell of green;
So I, who made her centre of my thought,
Became her worshipper; for when we know
The purity of that to which we bow
We grow sincere indeed. And she was all
That one might picture Eve to be when in
The slumber of her Paradise she woke,
And found herself within the clasp of flowers.

What wonder, then, if Agnes, yet a child,
Was to me all I wish'd for, that my life
Took half its being from the warmth of hers;
That all my motions were as if her eyes
Kept watch upon me; that my sleep became
The silent picture of the day, and set
The sweet rehearsal of my waking thoughts
Before me in the fairy hue of dreams;
That her sweet voice made all my pulses thrill,
While the light touch of her ethereal hand
Made the heart quicken, as beneath the shock
Of strangely started fears or open wrong.
O! love like this is worth ten years of all
The staider bearing of a sober manhood.
And if, perchance, we smile at all the warmth
Of boyish passion in those early days,
It reaches further than the lips, and in
The heart we feel the sadness living on,
Crown'd with the vain regret, the broken light
Of an existence only to be seen

Lighting some distant peak within the heart.
So I in Agnes found another life,
And felt the wonder of another land,
As if an angel had come down from heaven
To fill me with a little of his joy.
But did her eyes find out this love of mine,
And catch the worship which I wrapt her in ?
This was the question which I ask'd myself,
But found no fitting answer to reply;
For she partook so much of simple things,
And had such purity of thought and speech,
That if a thought of love had wing'd its flight
Across the open spaces of her heart,
It would have lost itself at once within
The fair fresh foliage of its innocent depths,
As when a bird will fly across a vale
And sink from sight amid a wealth of leaves.
Thus thought I, as the happy days flew on,
Flinging their sweetest light on me, until
A shadow fell upon my heart, and struck
The blossoms I had form'd, as when a hand
Strikes all unwittingly a feeble rose,
Whose leaves—full spent and ripe—fling down at once
Their rosy graces on the heedless ground.
For Agnes changed, and yet no change I knew,
But still it was a change, for which no name
Grew on the lip; a fear, a little touch
Of some soft warning, yet without its force.
But let me try to paint that one sweet day
We spent within the woods, before her strength
Grew a soft traitor, and confined her steps
To the hush'd precincts of her sacred room.

The sun was bright that day, and all the sky

Glimmer'd like magic with its sunniest light,
As if it knew that I, in later times,
Would look back on that fading light, and sigh,
And sadden at that splendour sunk in death.
We took our way along a path which kept
Our footsteps by a lake, wherein was seen
A little island dripping to the edge
With golden lilies, double in their bloom ;
When some, more amorous than the rest, leant o'er
And nodded to their shadows seen below.
The coot came forth at times to shew the speck
Of white upon his wings, then swept away
Behind the twisted roots. The silent heron,
Amid the tiny pillars of the reed,
Kept eager watch, nor stirr'd upon his post,
But stood a feather'd patience waiting prey ;
While in the woods the birds, as if ashamed
Of all their silence through the night, made up
The loss by one great gush of varied song,
Flooding all things, until the very leaves
Flutter'd to find a voice to vent their joy.
We heard the piping of the amorous thrush—
The bird that sings with all his soul in heaven—
The mellow blackbird, and the pert redbreast,
Whose song was bolder than his own bright eye ;
While fainter notes of lesser choristers
Came in like semitones to swell the whole ;
While over all, to crown this one great song,
The lark—the grey Apollo of his race,
The feather'd Pan, the spirit clad in song—
High up, and in the very sight of heaven,
Pour'd downward with the brightness of the smiles
Of angels all his spirit, leaving doubts
Whether his song belong'd to God or us.

And there we sat within the woods, and saw
The lake between the trees, and now and then
The gentle shadow of a cloud above
Passing along its bosom, as a thought
Across the calmness of a poet's brow.
And all around the lilies grew, and on
The bank beside us, rearing its sweet head,
The azure fairy of the woodland grass,
That has a spot of heaven for its eye,
The violet nestled, while, close by its side,
The primrose, yellow star of earth's green sky,
Peep'd up in bold surprise, and, further on,
An orchis, like the fiery orb of Mars,
Rose up with purple mouth agape to catch
All murmurs and all scents that came its way.

So in this Paradise we sat, until
We broke the silence with soft speech, to fit
The purer thought which, at the golden touch
Of the pure things beside us, grew within,
Blowing to instant blossom. Then our talk
Took simple bounds, and, with a fond delight,
We touch'd on all the heart will think, when youth
Ranges throughout its chambers; like to one
Who dares the sanctity of some fair room,
And finds in every corner fresh delight.
But I was bound by one great spell which she
Knew nothing of. I could not speak my love,
Nor could she see it, though in that sweet guise
In which we hide it only to be seen.

And so the converse sped—now quick at times,
Now slow, and then an interval in which
We went through all the paths of spoken thought,

Making the pleasure double by retouching
In silence the past interchange of words.
We felt the welcome of the summer day,
We heard its music rising everywhere;
Yet strange that all our thoughts should slip away
And strike a chord that beat not unison
With all this joy; for from our dreams and smiles
We shrunk, and, with a shadow in our eyes,
We struck upon the cypress'd edge of death.
Then solemn grew our converse, and she spoke
In low, sweet whispers, which to me were spells
Of deeper quiet, as she strove to make
A land wherein a great world moves like ours
Distinct and clear to all the grosser eye;
And simple as herself she painted heaven.
She knew not, as she spoke, how all my heart
Follow'd her words, and hung upon their tones
Helpless, and with no wish to change the task,
But catch the eloquence of what she spoke,
For truth lives nowhere but in simple words.

I hear her voice again this very hour
Clear and distinct, as if the death it wore
Made it the clearer, even as two friends,
Apart from each, but with a lake between,
Will keep up converse, losing not a word,
Because the faithful waters lie between.

But let me to the end, nor lengthen out
This memory only for myself, for dreams
Bring to the dreamers only pain or joy.

In two weeks after all I held as sweet
And pure of Agnes was within the grave.

For since time found a being comes this truth,
The sweetest heart within the sweetest breast
Beats not a tune to gain the ear of death.
So Agnes died, as flowers will die when frost
Falls, ere the sun is up, upon their bloom;
Or when some curious hand will open up
The undeveloped bud, that by its hue
The eye may picture forth the perfect flower.
Thus into the great garden of this life
Came death, and, lighting with an eager eye
Upon the bud I thought would bloom for me,
He prest aside the leaves that hid as yet
The glorious promise of a glorious flower,
Letting its unripe fragrance sink and die,
And so despoil'd it; leaving unto me
The scatter'd leaves to gather up at will.
So Agnes went away, when all her life
Stood like a prophet, mixing in its cup
Rare hopes, and novel tasks, and gentle things;
And just as she had raised it to her lips
To touch the golden nectar, lo! it fell
In rainbow pieces at her stricken feet;
And from the fragments lying now in dust,
As jewels glimmer through the barren sand,
Have I shaped out this sacred memory
Of her who rose upon my young pure life
First planet there, as in the midnight sky
A meteor lingers till it grasps the sight,
Then fades behind the fretwork of the stars.

CHATEAUX EN ESPAGNE.

IT is a pleasant thing to rhyme,
    Providing it but bring you money;
But sweeter still to pass the time
    In building fabrics high and sunny.
Alnaschar, ere he bent his knee
    To give a climax to his lecture,
Could by no chance have mated me
    At atmospheric architecture.

From early boyhood I began
    To follow Vathek, and erected
A goodly pile, upon a plan
    That was not with due care inspected.
I rear'd up columns rich with fret,
    And all the cunning of the gilder;
But somehow, to my deep regret,
    They always fell upon their builder.

I rear'd in many a forest black
    Huge castles by deep moats defended;
And strode their master, mail on back,
    With half-a-dozen knights attended.
We sat, like those of Branksome Hall,
    In armour, just as we were able,
And drank red wine from goblets tall,
    And clash'd mail'd hands across the table.

From this you cannot fail to guess
    That I was with the Middle Ages,

And never was at ease unless
  With stately dames and graceful pages.
But what with manhood sober'd down,
  Those dreams that made me so despotic
Have burst their chrysalis, and flown,
  And left me others less Quixotic.

And now, when in my building mood,
  And all my whims have free expansion,
I shape within a sober wood
  An old discolour'd Gothic mansion.
You scarce can see it for the trees
  That kindly interlace their branches,
Through which the sunshine slips at ease,
  And falls in sunny avalanches.

Around are long and shady walks,
  That lead in many a quaint direction—
Fit haunts for sage who sighs and talks,
  And shakes his head as in dejection;
Or some bold poet, when his thought
  Was at its swiftest mood for seizing
The glowing images it sought,
  And mould them into something pleasing.

Clear leaping fountains here and there
  Through all the summer day are playing;
Soft winds are coming through the air,
  That bring sweet incense in their straying.
And statues from the Greek are set—
  Aglow with all their snowy graces—
In nooks where drooping leaves are met,
  And half conceal them in their places.

But in my own sweet sanctum, where
    No outer noise dare make intrusion,
You ought to pay a visit there,
    And see the poet in seclusion.
The rich light falls upon the wall,
    Then fades away to something fainter,
Before white marble busts, and all
    The masterpieces of the painter.

Here as you enter, on your left
    A Goethe stands, whose marble vision
Seems still to keep that light which cleft
    Through all this life with such precision.
While on your right, with upturn'd brow,
    A Schiller stands, with noble presence,
To teach one all the upward glow
    Revolving round the purer essence.

Then right before me where I sit
    A Milton looks across to Dante,
Whose brows contract, as loth to fit
    The slender sprig of laurel scanty.
These two would always catch my eye
    When looking up for inspiration,
And teach me, when the mood was high,
    To mould the keen imagination.

In every nook within the room
    My favourite books get sacred lodgment—
Word-webs from the brain's restless loom,
    Spun out with truth and sober judgment.
A hundred spirits there repose,
    Who, at my slightest will and pleasure,

As Ariel did at Prospero's,
    Kneel down and offer up their treasure.

Like Southey, all my days would be
    Among the dead, but that is lying;
The mighty dead, it seems to me,
    Are those that only are undying.
Of course they take our death, a pain
    Which we, as humankind, inherit,
And pass for ever, to remain
    Swift's *struldbrugs* living in the spirit.

But I digress. Not all alone
    Am I within this learnèd palace,
For, as the twilight wanders on
    And feels along the distant valleys,
The door creeps softly back, and then
    A fairy creature growing bolder
Comes in, and, soft as falling rain,
    Lays both her hands upon my shoulder.

Then turning round, I see a face
    Where love with rounded youth is blended,
And all the nameless winning grace,
    Above my own all softly bended;
And, ere I can get time to speak,
    Or smile a welcome at the meeting,
Two little lips, all coy and meek,
    Against my own press rosy greeting.

Then, sitting on my knee, she slips
    One arm around me, while the other
Comes down, until her finger tips
    Are in my beard to plague and bother.

And still she whispers, while her look
    Turns sad to see my deep abstraction—
"Come, take a rest, your last new book
    Might surely give you satisfaction."

But just as I put up my hand
    To bring her head a little nearer,
To kiss the lips that so command,
    And tell her she is growing dearer—
Beim himmel! swift as lightning flies,
    My statues, mansion, wife, and fountains
Dissolve, and I—I rub my eyes,
    Like Rip Van on the Kaatskill mountains.

And so, instead of all my fame,
    My pictures, busts—both Greek and Roman—
A wife, a noble after-name,
    Which makes its owner envy no man;
Instead of running into town
    To see the last new book or picture,
Or hear some oracle full grown
    Deliver philosophic stricture:

In lieu of this, a case of books,
    A little room confined and narrow,
That might have sour'd the anxious looks
    Of Faust, whose thoughts eat to the marrow.
A little desk, where all my brains
    Get warp'd with long Parnassian creepers,
And dull'd throughout the day by trains,
    Pick, shovel, hammers, rails, and sleepers.

IN TEMPE.

'TWAS a shepherd in the Tempean vale,
   I heard Apollo play,
And send sweet music, like a lover's tale,
   Throughout the golden day.

I, too, not wishing to remain as mute,
   In happy fits essay'd
To finger with rude touch the piping lute;
   I touch'd it, but I made

Discordant music, jarring the nice ear
   Of dryad, nymph and faun,
Who, coming from their woodland haunts to hear,
   Back to their covert ran.

And now and then above me a white cloud
   Would open, and display
Some idle god therein, who laugh'd aloud,
   Then slowly moved away.

But ever as Apollo touch'd his lyre,
   Within me there upsprung
A longing for high music—a desire
   For something to be sung.

And this faint, sweet desire was sure to come
   In pauses, when aside
He flung his lyre to listen to the hum
   Of summer life. I tried

In such still intervals what mine would do,
  In simple wishfulness
To hear soft piping; all the discord grew
  Within it less and less.

And playing on, I smiled to hear its tone
  Coming so soft and sweet;
At times, too, when I thought myself alone
  I smiled in self-conceit.

But when I laid my lute aside to dream,
  Half seen before the eye
Sweet rural things, as bright as some stray beam,
  Would gently wander by.

Or lay themselves beside my feet in rest,
  Looking up with sweet eyes,
Whose light shot languor through my idle breast,
  Like sunbeams from the skies.

Above my head the green and tremulous leaf
  Ran music through my dreams,
Which brought no shadow, or stray touch of grief.
  Close by my feet the streams

Scarce stirr'd the pebbles. All was one great trust:
  The quick hours softly flew,
Flinging from golden spotted wings light dust
  That fell as soft as dew

On half-shut eyelids making-dreams upstart,
  Till the delighted eye
Reel'd in the sense of its creative art,
  As stars reel in the sky.

IN TEMPE.

Sometimes a goddess, hid in veils of light,
    Came downward from a cloud,
Shedding around her such a wild delight,
    I almost spoke aloud.

Then, half unveiling, she would show a limb
    White as the statue's snow,
And one ripe breast, at which my soul would swim,
    And all the pulses glow.

But when she bent her head till its red bud
    Lay crush'd against my cheek,
My spirit reel'd in fire throughout my blood,
    And rashly I would speak.

Then the dream faded; others came, in which
    I sat in high abodes,
With Hebe and her nectar within reach,
    And all the mighty gods.

I breath'd within the shadow of their light,
    Having no human care;
But bathing in continual delight
    With the Immortals there.

Wild passion-gusts were mine, I could not shun
    In that Olympian clime,
But met them with those throbs that melt and run
    Through Swinburne's sensuous rhyme.

For through that cloudless day a tinge of fire
    Ran, touching everything,
Making quick tongues that craved for sweet desire
    And all its nourishing.

Such were my visions in the Tempean vale,
    As day and night I lay
Hearing Apollo send a plaintive wail
    Of melody alway.

I heard the wild world's din afar, nor cared
    To hear its stirring sound;
Dreaming not that its labour must be shared
    Through all its reach and bound.

But idly sat, and ate the lotus leaf,
    Losing the nobler touch
Of that which makes us count one aim the chief,
    Which makes the rest a crutch.

But lo! a sudden voice came, as is heard
    The far, faint thunder's roar,
Crying—"O thou whose soul is never stirr'd
    To take the upward soar

With mankind, ever striving to work on,
    Spurr'd on by needs and wants,
Not listening, half asleep, to some stray tone
    For which the weak heart pants:

If thou hast aught in common with thy kind,
    Come from this idle mood,
And stand with willing heart and steadfast mind,
    As the brave worker should.

Hearest thou not the great world's mighty cry—
    'Lo, here is work for men!'
The deep, reverberating years reply,
    And answer back again."

With this voice ever ringing in my ear,
    I flung my lute away;
Came forth, and stood, half given up to fear,
    In all the open day.

I saw my fellows, brown'd and rough with toil,
    Work with all good in view;
And pushing onward with continuous moil
    To what is grand and true.

So, rising from my idle life, I took
    Tools that are fit for men,
And wrought and sung with brow inclined to brook
    No idle dream again.

And working on, new strength grew up in me,
    Such as when some new hope
Sends light into the heart, and we can see
    Clouds clearing from the scope.

This strength, too, led me on to other things
    That brought a clearer view;
I drank from the full source of purer springs,
    And framed myself anew.

I saw a better meaning, like sweet light
    Resting upon the earth,
Which led me with sure footstep to the right,
    With the old life a dearth

Within me, giving place to the high mind,
    Like mist to the sun's beam;
While Tempe and its vale lies far behind,
    Like an unfinish'd dream.

ALEXIS.

"He saw through his own soul."—Tennyson.

ALEXIS grew up, and through all his youth
    Ran dreams and splendours, as a summer bow
Lighting upon two hills uprears its arch
Against the clouds, and all the space below
Lies warm within its shadow : So his life,
Beneath such dreams, took golden hues of light,
And beat in wonder. He was yet a child,
Standing upon the flower-grown edge of life,
Yearning for manhood, which was seen afar,
Half-veil'd in shadow. Eager looks he cast
Before him to that wonder-land, which sent
Sweet echoes onward, that, to his rapt ear,
Were perfect music. To his soul within,
Expanding like a bud, these sounds became
Sure guides, that led his glowing thoughts away
To sunny regions, where the Beautiful,
Armida-like, sat canopied with roofs
Of dazzling golden fretwork. Life to him
Was the pure surface of a glossy shell,
Seen with the eye, but felt with no rough touch.
He knew not mankind, for the gift that looks
Beneath, and shapes from word and look the key
To open beings, was not his. He stood
A dreamer in the land of dreams, nor felt
The world jar with their action, but like one
Who feels himself drawn into some delight
And cannot turn, he went, and all the way
He had the unseen company of song,
Which, like low breathings coming from the sea,

Touch'd him to a new being, and he smiled
To think the gods had, in their idle moods,
Leant from their windless halls to touch his lips
With consecrating fire and make him sing—
A working priest of song amid his kind.
And with this thought there came to open up
His life a vision of high fame, as in the night
When the swift lightning runs a fiery track
To earth, and all the night grows white with fear:
So in Alexis rose the sudden hope
Of what might be when all this office fill'd
With the pure reaching forward of the thought
Which makes the poet; energies which strive,
Like some impulsive touch of God's, to shape
A higher life, which he forecasts himself,
And works out as he sings, still looking back
To see if any follow. Thus in him
There was continual bud and bloom, as in
A wood that slopes to catch the first of spring,
When unseen angels open up the flowers,
And bid them turn their clear wet eyes to God.
Fancies were his that like strong sunlight made
Within his heart the prints of joy and love,
As angels' footsteps print the floor of heaven.
So he grew up, and everywhere he found
A wealth of friends, who smiling seem'd to him
The early reflex of those times when truth
Was uppermost—the strength and soul of speech.
He bent himself to all their wish, he found
A pleasure in forestalling purpose, took
Words as a pledge for the fair truth, and smiled
To see the earth roll back to all its plan.
Then fell across his path a brighter beam,
From which his heart drank sweeter melody,

As when a sunbeam falls across a brook,
And gives a lighter music to its sound.
And she, the maiden who upon his life
Came like a wave of sunshine, as it slips
Along a field rich with the look of May,
Was fair and beautiful, and her sweet eyes
Look'd like a spirit's but half an hour in heaven.
What rapture was within him when he saw
This maiden rising up through all his dreams
To crown the inmost thoughts within his soul.
What worship shook his heart, when all the earth
Rose up, like some great organ, in whose tone
He heard the prelude to his life—we know
But cannot utter; for our deepest thoughts
Are known but to ourselves, and will not take
The garb of words. This much we know, that she
Glided throughout his life in light and love,
As down the Ganges floats the steady light
Of one frail lamp, still telling those who watch
Far off upon the bank that all is well.
He now was in the higher bounds, wherein
The early meaning of the glorious earth
Was half unveil'd, and in his soul there stirr'd
A sweet unrest, that was so sweet to him;
He wish'd no other for his paradise.
This was the golden summer of his life,
The mirror of his being, in whose light
He saw the very gods pass on with smiles
And music, leaving in their odorous tracks
The incense of Olympus. What to him
Was all the daily life of living men,
The custom and the course of earthly things?
He saw them not, for like the flower that turns
Its blossoms to the sun it follows still,

So all the thoughts and visions of the soul
Turn'd to that maiden, who for ever stood
Before him, the divinest of all things
That God hath sent into this world of ours.

We pause before we touch the other life,
To dream again the dreams Alexis dreamt ;
For life moves on in change, but still the heart
Turns to the softer as the purest, best.
And thus at times our own will muse, and think
Upon Alexis, and his dreams that were
So purely fashion'd ; and the new-found song
That in his bosom leapt, as when a stream
Slips down a few feet into foam, and makes
A summer music. These were sunny spots
Lighting upon his life, as when the hills
Lie in a gauze of mist, and through the clouds
Patches of sunlight, God's own gardening, falls.

He stood blindfolded with his dreams, until
The rude fact coming, with unsparing hand,
Snatch'd at the bandage which, unloosen'd, fell,
And left him face to face with sterner life.
O ! the harsh truth that must be learn'd with tears
By those who stand a step within the pale
Of life's strange mysteries. As a towering tree,
Struck by a sudden blight, though yet in prime,
Shakes, at the sudden breathing of a wind,
Its leaves from branches shrunk and dry, so at
The shock of real life all the golden thought
Fell off, and left him with a naked heart
To front the rough world with. He stood and saw
His life-dreams lying at his very feet
Shrunk into ashes ; for the one high idol

He worshipp'd, took the common form of earth,
And dwindled into a mere human shape,
Laying aside divinity as one
Flings off cast clothing. All those attributes
Which he, as pilgrims deck the shrine of saints,
Had given to that maiden, fell away,
Leaving her Lamia-like to stand and prick
His dreams, until, like other human things,
They warr'd upon each other. Then he turn'd
As one may who has fought for years to reach
His life's aim but to fail, and turn away
A calm face but a bleeding heart within,
The world not heeding of it. Then his life
Fell into gaps and chasms he could not step
Or even bridge, and in him the dislike
For fellowship rose up, and made his heart
A hermit in the breast, nor gave himself
To aims and purposes that work with men,
Drawing them on and up. He made himself
An adept in tongue-fence, and stung with words
The lighter fools around him. Out of this
He made a kind of armour, under which
He found such shelter that they let him pass,
Dreading its sting. But still with this there came,
From the night-time that lay around his heart,
Voices that whisper'd higher things, and sent
A yearning through his being, felt as yet
Like idle sounds that strike upon the ear
When one lies in the shade for summer heat,
Feeling around the edges of a dream.
But from this sting and idle quip of tongue,
As only fit for those who deftly move
Small puppets at a village fair, he turn'd,
And made himself the guest of other minds

In other language. He was strangely stirr'd
To find the same young worship in their hearts,
The same fond idols lying in the dust,
Like broken masterpieces of dead times
When gods had temples : then the fire and heat
Of all their youth-time, sinking down to warm
The roots of manhood, growing out to flower
In high endeavour. It may be that this,
And the contagion shooting from the soul
(For all true souls·stand girt in their own heat,
Warming all those who stand within it), made
Alexis find his depth, and shape his life
In other channels. In those noble ones
Who stereotype themselves in words he found
The aspirations and the high desire
To make the human take celestial shape,
And stand a little nearer to the gods.
So this grew in him also, as a bud
Swaying beneath the love-sigh of the spring
Swells out the livelong day, until he found
The looking backward not for any life
Upon this earth. He flung away those dreams
Which lay within the past, as when a rainbow
Fades, leaving one small speck against a cloud,
Pledge of its disappearance, and rose up
To battle manlike—to do what he could
To help his fellows, having in his heart
Those words of Goethe—" One should know his fellows,
And knowing also learn not to despise"—
A higher wisdom still.
    So there is now
In this Alexis better thought in germ
To meet the future with. For from his life
The noonday glare has fled, and left behind

The quieter light that draws the eye, as when
We stand and for a moment face the sun,
Seeming to sink between the hill and sky,
Then turn to view the chasten'd light behind—
Faint harbinger of twilight. Life to him
Has half unveil'd its meaning, and he sees
No puppet show to make a wrinkle live
About the lip and eye, but earnest work
For earnest men, within whose band must be
No dainty worker, gloved, and ever strong
In idle words, but bare-arm'd fighters, swift
To take advantage of the rising ground
And wave their fellows onward. He has learnt,
Though he is yet what some call young, that men
Are ever to be on this miraculous earth
To make it better, working hand and brain
To lift it higher, standing firm of foot,
Shoulder to shoulder, striving for all good,
And keeping God and duty in the eye,
As sailors keep the light that marks their port
For guide and haven. Shame on him if he
Should stand an idle Memnon in the crowd,
Giving responses to each one who strikes,
For the mere whim of hearing sound, and thus
Be jester to his fellows, as a mother
May hum a cradle-song to please her child
Fretful with sleep. What need of nursery rhyme
In this great age of sounding wire and wheel,
Science and all her handmaids? Rather toil,
And manly living, manly thought, and all
Those grander interests ever moving on
To where we strive for. Crude and vaguely dim
Is this life of Alexis yet, but still
It rises slowly upward, as the moon

Bound in a slip of crescent rises up
And shines a silver sickle in the sky.
He may fail in the task of working out
What he has laid before him as a plan,
And sink before the crescent culminates
And shines an orb, as vessels sink at sea,
Reaching no port. But now he tears away
The dreamer from his being, calling out
To all his fellows (for in him the wish
To see them reach the purer heights of life
Shoots from the rest, and claims his deepest thought,
As high hills claim the sun) to rise and take
The nobler pathway, working on and up;
Not resting, though the sweat be in our eyes
Blinding our motions, till the brute be shorn
From out our being, and we stand erect,
The earth beneath our feet, the sky above,
And right before us all the nobler path
That narrows not as earthly pathways do,
But ever broadens as it reaches up
Until it ends beside the feet of God.

TO AN OLD SCHOOLFELLOW.

"Der Schulfreund wird nie vergessen."—*Jean Paul.*

YOUR Edinburgh is well enough—
    Stone picture of the past and present;
But we have in us better stuff
    To make the winter evening pleasant.
So doff your heavy coat and hat,
    And let the nipping winds still bellow,

We'll poke the fire, and have a chat
  Across the table, old schoolfellow.

Your Darnleys, Bothwells, what are they
  To make us weep the modern fashion?
The former was of ductile clay,
  The latter rough and strong with passion.
And Mary—here I bend the eye,
  For, hang it, I am weak and human,
And pay my homage in a sigh
  To her, the royal queen and woman.

Of course it is but right to talk
  About your Scott and all those fellows,
Who stand the cock of their own walk,
  And make us halting rhymsters jealous.
Your fine De Quincey and Kit North,
  Keen critic, pugilist, and better,
Yet won a belt of golden worth
  In the keen struggle of *belles lettres*.

But not of these shall we discourse;
  To-night we pour a rich libation
To all the past, and put in force
  A retrospective conversation.
So draw a little closer, Joe,
  We'll let our manhood slip the tether,
And walk into the long ago,
  When we were at the school together.

You still remember the old school,
  In which we sat with eye discerning,
And head of solemn wisdom full—
  Two infant Solomons of learning.

TO AN OLD SCHOOLFELLOW.

How prim and staid we tried to look,
　　Like wisdom's owl from out our places;
Then bit the cover of our book,
　　And tried our hand at making faces.

Then grew up to its highest strength
　　The palmy state of flagellation,
And brought to us the wish at length
　　To make some dire recrimination.
But still (for tears came ready then)
　　We stretch'd out hands with many a whimper,
Yet Traddles-like, when all the pain
　　Had pass'd we straight began to simper.

But do you mind that day of dread,
　　When all at once our old gray master
Put up his spectacles and said—
　　"These boys!" and then his speech grew faster,
Till, ere we could be fairly mute,
　　He came, and out not one he singled,
But thrash'd us all from dux to foot,
　　Till every tiny sinner tingled?

But we were worthy of it then;
　　For what with killing Lindley Murray,
And wasting paper, ink, and pen,
　　We kept him in a constant worry.
We fought, too, Joe, as boys will fight
　　When in their little heats of passion;
But in two minutes made it right,
　　And went about in loving fashion.

What pictures, too, of things we drew
　　Instead of sums our dirty slate on!

They might have given a hint or two
  To Holman Hunt or Noel Paton.
Our facile pencil, quick of touch,
  Sketch'd landscape, hamlet, cot, and city,
And narrow glens and caverns, such
  As offer shelter to banditti!

I drew the heroes of that age
  Now named the "iron," and I painted
Knights with their chargers in a rage,
  And warriors that now are sainted.
Hood speaks of his "art's early days,"
  And we, who are less worthy mortals,
May speak of ours, and claim some praise
  For serving at Apollo's portals.

But O! that happy time, when we
  Anticipated love's sweet fetters;
And like young Eupheists set free
  Our passion in a flight of letters.
You wrote to Mary; I to Kate;
  We gave our boyish lore an airing,
And hinted what would be our fate
  If they should go against our pairing.

I wonder where they are just now,—
  Those sweethearts of that tender season;
Will wifehood be upon their brow?
  A thing that plainly stands to reason.
If we could see them by the hearth—
  Who knows but such a thing yet may be?
They'd ask us, full of matron mirth,
  If we would like to nurse the baby.

Then I would give a stare or two,
    And make what answer I was able
By rising from my chair to view,
    Then lay my hand upon the table,
And stammer—" When I saw you last
    This was, I think, about your stature ;
But now—good heavens ! time flies fast,
    And you are in your wish'd-for nature."

But *verbum sat* upon that theme,
    This seems to me a poor digression ;
And why should we of sorrow dream,
    And give our thoughts a sad expression?
The happier part is ours to-night,
    So never let our thoughts turn yellow ;
But let our fancy have free flight
    As we sit talking, old schoolfellow.

What days were those when summer brought
    The long vacation, and the ramble
Through field and wood, in which we sought,
    Like the two babes, the glossy bramble ;
Or hung upon some branchy point,
    For nuts of brown and crimson lustre ;
And oft got sadly out of joint
    By fighting for the largest cluster !

We were two little Waltons then,
    Well skill'd in piscatory searches ;
And proudly show'd our finny gain,
    In trouts and porcupine-like perches.
No rocky hill or mossy ground
    To loch or streamlet could prevent us,

But off, with many a frisk and bound,
   We set, as if *non compos mentis*.

I still could point you out the pool
   By which you sat, with patience banded,
And never let your ardour cool
   Until your first small trout was landed.
I see the sparkle in your eye,
   The triumph upon every feature,
As with a sanguinary cry
   You kill'd the little trembling creature.

And then, when we had need of rest,
   We sat by each, and, all-confiding,
Exchanged what dreams were in our breast
   As to our future plan and guiding.
We were to be great men, and take
   High paths that all our kind would travel,
And live pure lives, and never make
   A slip at which our friends might cavil.

Ah me! those dreams are now no more,
   And we, since they have slipt their bridle,
Might well have sat as models for
   Some modern Hogarth's Thomas Idle.
But, *che importa*, we have had
   Our little spell at blowing bubbles;
And now, for I am turning sad,
   We have our manhood and its troubles.

The little hamlet where our sweet
   Swift boyhood sped knows not our faces;
Strange footsteps pace its little street,
   And other forms fill up our places.

Bowl'd out by life's remorseless aim,
    That will not let us keep our wicket,
We try our hand at labour's game,
    And find it other work than cricket.

So be it, Joe; our ups and downs
    Have left us, after all their pillage,
You in the drawing-room of towns,
    I coop'd up in a quiet village.
Yet here they have, in kindly part,
    Brought us this night once more together;
Two men in face, yet boys at heart,
    As when we went to school together.

" As when we went to school." Ah dear !
    We then were headstrong, slim, and sallow,
And like a Nelson had no fear,
    For we were careless, smooth, and callow.
But now (nay, never hide your beard,
    Here's one upon my chin to mate it),
We're rough and strong, and all prepared
    For that to which we may be fated.

And so your hand ! The past again
    Has made us draw a little nearer,
And look on aught that happen'd then
    As something yearly growing dearer.
For boyhood, like sweet love's first prime,
    Has spells that were divinely given;
And all the light that crown'd that time
    Fell somewhere from a rent in heaven.

Tush ! all this prating wearies you,
    Who care not for such backward fancies,

But hold them, like some bill just due,
   As things to start St Vitus dances.
You shake your head. I do you wrong;
   Well, if there's aught I can remember,
Why, Joe, I'll hitch it into song,
   And bore you with it next December.

A SONG OF PROGRESS.

COME away from pick and shovel for another day again,
   Glide along the veins of iron leading to the city's heart,
Walk its streets and rub a shoulder with my wondrous fellow-men,
   Then come back and stand with firmer foot in labour's toiling mart.

Thus I thought as ever onward, through the golden summer day,
   Went the engine, all his pathway ringing answers to his tread,
Heard him shriek at every fitful gleam of red that cross'd his way,
   His great nineteenth century watch-cry for the world to move ahead.

Ah! what toil in dark and daylight, aching brain and weary eye,
   Waiting for the magic thought to burst its cycled chrysalis,
Till at last, like some Messiah, Science brought her handmaids nigh,
   And we stood on stairs of centuries with a mighty thing like this!

He our wild familiar, tamed to rush where'er we point or speak,
   Turning, where his footsteps wander, earth into one mighty mart;
Looming in the midst of traffic, as from out the ranks of Greek
   Tower'd the elephant, striking terror into every Roman's heart.

A SONG OF PROGRESS.

Lo! at last the toiling city, where the foremost ranks of life
    Rush and strive in ceaseless struggle, ebbing but to come again;
And my heart leaps up within me, palpitating for the strife,
    In the maelstrom of swart traffic, in the toil and shock of men.

Here is life on either hand that might disturb each idle god—
    Drowsy-brain'd, with golden nectar bubbling from Hebean cup:
Life, as if some mighty giant had beneath these streets abode,
    And was stretching every muscle in his frenzy to burst up.

Shame on all the later devil's whisper, crying in our ear—
    "We are apes of broader forehead, with the miracle of speech;"
Rather nineteenth century men, that have a thought Who sent us here:
    Higher faiths are ours, my fellows, low enough for us to reach.

What though I, your feeble helpmate, stand among you all unknown?
    Yet each pulse within me, as a hand laid on responsive strings,
Vibrates to each new-shaped purpose rising up within your own,
    Ringing forth excelsior pæans for the onward march of things.

Everywhere to bound the vision, the miraculous faith of toil
    Rears, as worship, mighty monsters with their hundred arms flung loose;
Miles of vessels throbbing in their haste to fling a liquid coil
    Of commerce round the nations kneeling with their proffer'd use.

What a seven-leagued stride from Adam, and the languor of the East,
    To this century lapping round us, like a mad and hungry sea,
To the chainless brain that, like the geni, from the dark released,
    Fills the earth with triumphs, earnest of the greater yet to be.

Heavens! how the unseen multitudinous Laocoöns of thought
   Draw this earth within their clasp, till, as upon the father's face,
Where the Deity of pain grew, as the throbbing sculptor wrought,
   So her rugged features lighten, lying in their coil'd embrace.

But I wander from the city. Let me turn again to find
   In the waves of human faces rolling past on either side
Links that, strong as bands of iron, draw me onward to my kind,
   Till their fellowship shoots through me with electric thrills of pride.

For in them is the sure seed from which the ages yet to be,
   Rising up with great broad sickle, shall reap all its golden grain;
Then the kindlier thought and nobler use of manhood shall be free,
   And be brighter from the struggle such a sunny height to gain.

This we may not see; yet, brothers, it were something grand to die
   But to hear a shout ring upward, through the death-mists thick and vast,
Loud as when a thousand people join their voice in one long cry,
   That the world's great fight for brotherhood had clutch'd the palm at last.

It will come: I hear its promise ringing on from street to street
   (Shame if we could play for ever at the game of Hoodman-blind):
I can see it; other mark than Cain's upon each brow I meet;
   And the engine's whistle shrieks it as the city sinks behind.

Back to honest pick and shovel, and to daily task again—
   Back with nobler thoughts within me, all the higher aims to cheer;
Better, too, in having rubb'd a shoulder with my fellow-men,
   And the thinking that I help them at my lowly labour here.

LIVINGSTONE.

BRING him to England, for the goal is won;
 The grand old man, whose soul was as a spark
From the great force of God, has nobly run
 His life path, dying at the very mark.

Lo! the quick wires flash out their news, and look
 How the deep nature of our sympathy
Wells up in sorrow that no bar can brook
 For him whose name is for the years to be!

His is no paltry fading laurel bough,
 No trophy when the useless fight is o'er,
But one green wreath of brotherhood is now
 Girt round these toil-seam'd brows for evermore.

Noble to be like him, so firm of heart,
 Pressing still forward, dragging on behind
The electric chain of fellowship to start
 The same high feeling for our swarthier kind.

God-like his mission, and I count him one,
 The gray-hair'd man, within whose large deep breast
A giant's soul beat till his task was done,
 And, overwearied, he himself took rest.

We mourn not all alone; from those far lands
 Where faces that, though dark, still show their tears,
Comes the sharp cry for help, and swarthy hands
 Waving to us in all their hopes and fears.

We still have many props to lean upon,
    But where shall they, our dusky brethren, seek
(Their pillar, Samson-like, by Death o'erthrown),
    For one to take his work, and guide and speak?

The loss is theirs. And yet what mighty fruit
    Will spring from it in the far coming time?
What tendrils from this man will grow and shoot
    From heart to heart, and on from clime to clime?

Lo! as the years come, with their peace or strife,
    I see each handful of their earnest men
Pause, and kneel down by this heroic life,
    Till all its fervour makes them strong again.

And so hereafter (for we dare not name
    Marble to him) he shall, in noble light,
Stand between two worlds apart, and by one claim
    Lay dusky brother hands within the white.

Bring him to England, then—no other land
    Shall offer Africa's apostle rest;
There lay him down, the noblest of that band
    Who have God's very nature in their breast.

BY THE GRAVE OF LIVINGSTONE.

Das Tüchtige wenns wahrhaft ist,
Wirkt über alle zeiten hinaus.—Goethe.

LET there be fingers on the lips to-day,
    And footsteps check'd to a less hasty tread;
Let human reverence reach its highest sway
    While England gathers in her noble dead.

Yes! we bring one to swell the mighty throng
  Of those who ever planet-like are seen—
Fire pillars in war, in politics, in song,
  Or where this boundless breadth of thought has been.

And he for whom we claim this high, meet place
  Comes heralded by ours—a nation's tears;
Asking with mute, worn, death-ennobled face,
  A kindly union with his fellow peers.

If toil and struggle for fraternal right
  Can grant this boon: If work for brother men,
And firm endurance and heroic might,
  That fought the long battle of this life again:

If the old faith in God, and all that hope
  Which, like a sunbeam through the winter gloom,
Flashes through doubts and shadows till they ope—
  Then give this gray-worn martyr rest and room.

Lo! as they bring him on the ages rise,
  And in far whispers, like the boundless wind,
Cry, "He is only greatest in our eyes
  Who toils and conquers for his fellow-kind."

And that far whisper, as the sunshine slips,
  Broad-wing'd and fleet, from summer hill to hill,
Echoes through worlds, and, lighting on the lips,
  Quickens the soul to higher standard still:

For men are ever noble when they stand
  In sovereign worship of some kingly one,
Who toil'd for them with brain, and foot, and hand,
  Till death came, and the godlike task was done.

His, too, is finish'd ; but, before the dust
    Be hidden, let us look upon this man,
That his life energy and tireless trust
    May be ours also as we work our span.

Ye, too, whose life-paths in this world are dim—
    Who see no finger-posts in earth or sky—
Come, and see clearer as ye gaze on him,
    And learn how man may nobly live and die.

But speech is idle. Better in this hour,
    When England waits to clasp him to her breast,
That silence speak our grief with better power
    Than the loud sorrow as he sinks to rest.

Then lay him down, not with that pomp or state
    Which follows kings—though he, too, wore a crown
Upon that brow—but with strong England's great
    All solemnly and simply lay him down.

There let him rest, while the great ages roll,
    Reaping the harvest which his hand has sown.
Thou noble worker of the grand, firm soul,
    Thou pioneer of brotherhood, sleep on !

BLOOD ON THE WHEEL.

"BLESS her dear little heart!" said my mate, and he pointed out to me,
Fifty yards to the right, in the darkness, a light burning steady and clear.
"That's her signal in answer to me, when I whistle, to let me see
She is at her place by the window the time I am passing here."

I turn'd to look at the light, and I saw the tear on his cheek—
He was tender of heart, and I knew that his love was lasting and strong—
But he dash'd it off with his hand, and I did not think fit to speak,
But look'd right ahead through the dark, as we clank'd and thunder'd along.

They had been at the school, the two, and had run, like a single life,
Through the mazes of childhood up to the sweeter and firmer prime,
And often he told me, smiling, he had promised to make her his wife,
In the rambles they had for nuts in the woods in the golden autumn time.

"I must make," he would add, "that promise good in the course of a month or two;
And then, when I have her safe and sound in a nook of the busy town,
No use of us whistling then, Joe, lad, as now we incline to do,
For a wave of her hand, or an answering light as we thunder up and down."

Well, the marriage was settled at last, and I was to stand by his side,
Take a part in the happy rite, and pull from his hand the glove;

And still as we joked between ourselves, he would say, in his manly
    pride,
    That the very ring of the engine-wheels had something in them
        of love.

At length we had just one run to make before the bridal took place,
    And it happen'd to be in the night, yet merry in heart we went on;
    But long ere he came to the house, he was turning each moment
        his face
        To catch the light by the window, placed as a beacon for him alone.

"Now then, Joe," he said, with his hand on my arm, "keep a
    steady look out ahead
    While I whistle for the last time;" and he whistled sharply and
        clear;
    But no light rose up at the sound; and he look'd with something
        like dread
        On the white-wash'd walls of the cot, through the gloom looking
            dull, and misty, and drear.

But lo! as he turn'd to whistle again, there rose on the night a scream,
    And I rush'd to the side in time to catch the flutter of something
        white;
    Then a hitch through the engine ran like a thrill, and in haste he
        shut off the steam,
        While we stood looking over at each with our hearts beating
            wild with affright.

The station was half a mile ahead, but an age seem'd to pass away
    Ere we came to a stand, and my mate, as a drunken man will reel,
    Rush'd on to the front with his lamp, but to bend and come back
        and say,
        In a whisper faint with its terror—"Joe, come and look at this
            blood on the wheel."

Great heaven! a thought went through my heart like the sudden stab of a knife,
  While the same dread thought seem'd to settle on him and palsy his heart and mind,
For he went up the line with the haste of one who is rushing to save a life,
  And with the dread shadow of what was to be I follow'd closely behind.

What came next is indistinct, like the mist on the mountain side—
  Gleam of lights and awe-struck faces, but one thing can never grow dim:
My mate, kneeling down in his grief like a child by the side of his mangled bride,
  Kill'd, with the letter still in her hand she had wished to send to him.

Some little token was in it, perhaps to tell of her love and her truth,
  Some little love-errand to do ere the happy bridal drew nigh;
So in haste she had taken the line, but to meet, in the flush of her fair sweet youth,
  The terrible death that could only be seen with a horror in heart and eye.

Speak not of human sorrow—it cannot be spoken in words;
  Let us veil it as God veil'd His at the sight of His Son on the cross.
For who can reach to the height or the depth of those infinite yearning chords
  Whose tones reach the very centre of heaven when swept by the fingers of loss?

She sleeps by the little ivied church in which she had bow'd to pray—
  Another grave close by the side of hers, for he died of a broken heart,

Wither'd and shrunk from that awful night like the autumn leaves
   in decay,
And the two were together that death at first had shaken so
   roughly apart.

But still, when I drive through the dark, and that night comes
   back to my mind,
I can hear the shriek take the air, and beneath me fancy I feel
The engine shake and hitch on the rail, while a hollow voice from
   behind
   Cries out, till I leap on the footplate, "Joe, come and look at
   this blood on the wheel!"

JENNY WI' THE AIRN TEETH.

WHAT a plague is this o' mine,
   Winna steek his e'e,
Though I hap him ow'r the head
   As cosie as can be.
Sleep! an' let me to my wark,
   A' thae claes to airn;
Jenny wi' the airn teeth,
   Come an' tak' the bairn:

Tak' him to your ain den,
   Where the bowgie bides,
But first put baith your big teeth
   In his wee plump sides;
Gie your auld grey pow a shake,
   Rive him frae my grup—

Tak' him where nae kiss is gaun
When he waukens up.

Whatna noise is that I hear
Comin' doon the street?
Weel I ken the dump-dump
O' her beetle feet.
Mercy me, she's at the door,
Hear her lift the sneck;
Whisht! an' cuddle mammy noo
Closer roun' the neck.

Jenny wi' the airn teeth,
The bairn has aff his claes,
Sleepin' safe an' soun', I think—
Dinna touch his taes;
Sleepin' weans are no for you;
Ye may turn about
An' tak' awa' wee Tam next door—
I hear him screichin' oot.

Dump, dump, awa' she gangs
Back the road she cam';
I hear her at the ither door,
Speirin' after Tam.
He' a crabbit, greetin' thing,
The warst in a' the toon;
Little like my ain wee wean—
Losh, he's sleepin' soun'.

Mithers hae an awfu' wark
Wi' their bairns at nicht—
Chappin' on the chair wi' tangs
To gi'e the rogues a fricht.

Aulder weans are fley'd wi' less,
   Weel aneuch, we ken—
Bigger bowgies, bigger Jennies,
   Frichten muckle men.

THE POET.

THE poet is not for the crowd; he stands
   An isolation from the multitude,
And breathes a breath which comes from higher lands,
   Where good rules over good.

He sees the unseen force of things that move
   In systems parallel to those of ours,
And widely grasps the universal love
   And law that rules the flowers.

So, warming with his given task, he flings
   The quietness of never-failing strength
Around all forms, till, Hercules-like, he brings
   The fire-eyed Truth at length:

And fencing her with sharp, keen words, she creeps
   Throughout the beating heart and mighty limb
Of this upheaving earth; and, if she sleeps,
   'Tis but to be like him

Who rests beneath his hill of fire, yet wakes
   With heaven-filling smoke and thunder sound:
So she, arising in word armour, shakes
   The universal bound.

He scans with lightning glance the great abyss,
    Wherein is laid the daily wrong and sin,
And whispers, "Bloodshed will not vanquish this—
    What if a song should win?"

Then, catching the swift hour, with fearless breast
    He sings. The foremost of the silent years
Shrinks in his shame that such a blot should rest
    Upon himself and peers.

And the quick words, swathed in their music, drop
    Like summer blossoms left by fickle winds,
And, taking root, spring up and flower, like hope
    In human hearts and minds:

That, feeling the new growth, start up to hear
    Murmurs within as of the waking soul,
And nerving whispers, full of strength and cheer,
    For the far heavenward goal.

So from the hurry of the world's great mart
    The poet stands, inviolate and strong,
Shooting, Apollo-like, his word-dipp'd dart
    Full in the front of wrong.

THE WORSHIP OF SORROW.

HE who, in his young sweet lifetime,
    When his heart with its visions was rife,
Hath felt not the worship of sorrow
    Lapping round the shores of that life:

Goes out to the toil of his fellows
    With no share in their hopes or their fears;
And can only stand at a distance,
    And see them weep their tears.

Nor hath he found out in the night-time,
    When his heart and himself were alone,
That each wondrous chord in their bosom
    Was an unseen link to his own,

And that every yearning within them,
    The manifold aim and desire,
Came along that link, as the message
    Is spoken in shocks through the wire.

It was thus in that past existence,
    With its purposeless unrest,
When the infinite nature of Sorrow
    Was clasping me breast to breast.

And I stood in the dim, hush'd twilight,
    While the rising tears made me blind,
As within, like a rain-quicken'd streamlet,
    Rose the hopes and fears of my kind.

I am now in my bearded manhood,
  And the finer perceptions then
Have roughen'd and dull'd in their feelings,
  Since I stood with my shoulder to men.

But still at stray times, when the labour
  And fret of the day is o'er,
That early worship comes backward,
  As a wave returns to the shore.

It comes when I stand in the silence
  On the bridge at the head of the town,
With the streamlet running beneath me,
  And the stars above looking down.

But most when I go to the city,
  And see upon either side
The restless hurry of faces
  That come and go like the tide.

For I know that each one in his bosom,
  Amid the toil and the din,
Has a goal set out in the future
  Which he braces himself to win.

And I also know, ere the struggle
  And the life-long conflict be o'er,
He must enter this temple of Sorrow,
  And worship, weary and sore.

For this mystical life around us,
  Like the earth, with its day and night,
Is a hope and a fear and a sorrow,
  Till we enter the purer light.

JAMIE'S WEE CHAIR.

THE snawdrap was oot, and the primrose was seen
　In the cleuch, while the side o' the burnie was green;
The mavis was heard singin' sweet in the wud,
While a safter licht fell frae the edge o' the clud;
The whaups an' the peasweeps skirl'd lood on the hill,
When the pride o' the hoose, oor wee Jamie, fell ill;
But lang ere that snawdrap had wither'd an' gane,
A wee grave was a' we had left o' oor wean.

'Twas an unco sair trial for baith John an' me,
For the bairnie was just the tae licht o' my e'e.
As for him, he scarce ken'd what he whiles wud be at,
Wi' his wee Jamie this and his wee Jamie that;
But that nicht when Death cam' in white licht owre his broo,
He said, takin' my han', "Jean, that's owre wi' us noo."
Then he sat down an' grat, cryin', half in despair,
"We hae naebody noo to fill Jamie's wee chair."

I bore up mysel', wi' the tear on my cheek,
An' the thochts in my heart that I couldna weel speak,
An' aften I took a step ben to the room
To kiss the wee lips that still keepit their bloom;
But at last, when the day cam' to tak' him away,
And the last o' the fouk was seen climbing the brae,
I cam' in frae the door, an' I grat lang an' sair,
Wi' my heid on the airm o' my Jamie's wee chair.

O, the bliss o' warm tears when the sair heart is fu',
Fa'in' saft on oor grief like kind Heaven's ain dew,

Till, as rain lowns the win', so the sorrow that fain
Wad rise up against God settles calmly again ;
An', as saft, siller cluds an' the wide, happy sky
Turn the brichter and bluer when storms hae gaen by,
Sae the gloom roun' my life lichten'd up everywhere
As I raise an' took ben my deid Jamie's wee chair.

Then I took doon the plaicks frae the shelf on the wa',
The whussle, the peerie, the pony, an' ba',
Put them safe in the drawer ; an', when I had dune,
The door saftly open'd, an' John steppit in.
He stood just awee, then began to look roun',
But stoppit on seein' the plaicks a' ta'en doon ;
Then he spier'd, his voice shakin' wi' grief mair an' mair,
" Jean, where hae ye puttin oor Jamie's wee chair ?"

I raise, as he spoke, frae the cheerless fire en',
Gaed into the room, brocht the chair quately ben,
Put it into its place, never liftin an e'e,
But sat doon, while John drew himsel' nearer to me ;
Then I fan' his braid han' tak' a grup o' my ain,
As he said, " Jean, it's a' for the sake o' the wean,
For ye ken weel aneuch that the bairn last sat there,
So atween us this forenicht we'll keep his wee chair."

We drew near the hearth, the tears fillin' oor een
As we sat han'-in-han' wi' the wee chair between ;
An' aye as we thocht on a bricht lauchin' face,
An' a curly bit heid noo nae mair in its place,
We turn'd, as if a' oor sair loss was a name,
An' wee Jamie wad juist be aside us the same.
O, it tak's unco schulin', and God's help an' care,
To mak' mithers believe in an empty wee chair.

We sat, while the hills creepit close in the nicht;
But the stars, lookin' doon, kent that a' wasna richt,
For they whisper'd to me o' a joy yet in store,
An' a something abune them I ne'er had afore.
I turn'd roun' to John, laid my han' on his knee,
As I tell't what the stars keepit sayin' to me;
Then we kneel'd down, oor hearts risin' up in a prayer,
As oor heids met aboon oor deid Jamie's wee chair.

Years hae gaen by since thaun, but still warm in oor heart
What the stars said has aye been fulfillin' its pairt;
An' we see noo that a' was intended for guid,
Though God's han' at the time by oor sorrow was hid;
But as rainbows are brichter against a black sky,
So God's meanin's grow clear when His shadow gangs by;
An' in a' the bit trials that fa' to oor share,
We aye keep atween us oor Jamie's wee chair.

EARLY POET LIFE.

O, HOW bright were those early summers
    When, like Heaven's own dazzling bow,
All the rapt, deep life of the poet
    Rose up with its wildest glow.

  When the quick, sweet rush of the fancy
      Came on me like a fairy crowd,
  Or a sudden gush of sunlight,
      Through the rift of an April cloud.

Then my heart took a deeper motion,
    As from stream and hill and tree
Came a music that bore in its cadence
    The sweetest of dreams to me.

Whispers, too, as when swaying grasses
    Bow down to the evening wind,
Were for ever thrilling my being
    With the touch of the wider mind.

Then the years that lay out before me
    Rose up in their height sublime,
Giving forth in oracular voices
    The promise of golden rhyme.

And my spirit at such sweet promise
    Leapt up in its wild delight,
Like the North light laying its fingers
    On the lips of the stars by night.

Nature wept in divinest secret
    The sweetest of tears on me,
Till I lost myself in the splendour
    Of the boundless good to be.

O, how bright were those early summers!
    Never come such moments now;
All that early madness has faded
    To a duller and paler glow.

Yet at times, like a flash of sunlight
    From the inmost depths of the heart,
The old, sweet yearnings spring upward
    That for want of words must depart.

But I whisper, " A greater triumph
   Is yet to be had with thy peers
Than the one that is cool'd with the laurel,
   Or a life in the front of the years.

Thou canst teach them in what of music
   Is left from that early song,
All the force that lies hid in their labour
   Like a saint's when his spirit is strong.

Thou canst teach them, too, that for ever,
   Like the waves that come again,
So over the world's rough bosom
   Flow the toiling races of men :

Who, in all their fighting and striving,
   With hearts that bid them be brave,
Are as types of the soul's high wrestle
   For other goals than the grave.

Yet, whatever thou sing, let thy lyrics
   Have something in them of cheer,
And a battle-word for the feeble
   Who sicken and weary here.

If thou sing not to them as they struggle,
   With the purpose of making them strong,
Then thou thyself art a traitor
   In the federation of song.

But if there be heard in thy music
   The fire and the true sphere tone,
That, striking within their bosoms,
   Makes a march to help them on :

Then sing with thy back to those summers,
And the wild quick flush of that time
When thy heart had no thought of its fellows
Or the sacred priesthood of rhyme."

CUDDLE DOON.

THE bairnies cuddle doon at nicht,
   Wi' muckle faucht an' din;
O, try and sleep, ye waukrife rogues,
   Your faither's comin' in.
They never heed a word I speak;
   I try to gie a froon,
But aye I hap them up, an' cry,
   "O, bairnies, cuddle doon."

Wee Jamie wi' the curly heid—
   He aye sleeps next the wa',
Bangs up an' cries, "I want a piece"—
   The rascal starts them a'.
I rin an' fetch them pieces, drinks,
   They stop awee the soun',
Then draw the blankets up an' cry,
   "Noo, weanies, cuddle doon."

But ere five minutes gang, wee Rab
   Cries oot, frae 'neath the claes,
"Mither, mak' Tam gie ower at ance,
   He's kittlin' wi' his taes."
The mischief's in that Tam for tricks,
   He'd bother half the toon;

But aye I hap them up an' cry,
  "O, bairnies, cuddle doon."

At length they hear their faither's fit,
  An', as he steeks the door,
They turn their faces to the wa',
  While Tam pretends to snore.
"Hae a' the weans been gude?" he asks,
  As he pits aff his shoon.
"The bairnies, John, are in their beds,
  An' lang since cuddled doon."

An' just afore we bed oorsel's,
  We look at oor wee lambs;
Tam has his airm roun' wee Rab's neck,
  An' Rab his airm roun' Tam's.
I lift wee Jamie up the bed,
  An' as I straik each croon,
I whisper, till my heart fills up,
  "O, bairnies, cuddle doon."

The bairnies cuddle doon at nicht
  Wi' mirth that's dear to me;
But sune the big warl's cark an' care
  Will quaten doon their glee.
Yet, come what will to ilka ane,
  May He who sits aboon
Aye whisper, though their pows be bauld,
  "O, bairnies, cuddle doon."

A SONG FOR MY FELLOWS.

"Ambos oder Hammer sein."—Goethe.

MY brothers, in this great world of ours
    Our hearts have need to be strong,
And have in them, like shady nooks in a wood,
    A shelter for stirring song.
So this snatch of wisdom from Goethe in mine
    Is for ever speaking to me,
In the battle of life, from birth unto death—
    "Thou must hammer or anvil be."

Hammer or anvil, so runs the rhyme,
    To beat or be beaten upon—
Whether thou stand in the first of the ranks,
    Or be left in the rear alone.
But shame on that coward who, faint in his heart,
    Would wish to slink from the fray,
Or could bend himself to each turn of the fight,
    As a potter might fashion his clay.

Other way must this daily battle be fought,
    With no craven heart in the breast,
But keeping keen eye on the colours ahead,
    And shoulder and pace with the rest.
The bravest of all the fighters is he
    Who, whatever chance may betide,
Can turn and fashion some battle-word
    For his fellows on either side.

Then, brothers, let us rise up from our fears,
    No anvils are we, but men

Who can wield the sledge-hammer, like mystic Thor,
    For the daily battle again.
Let us strike, with an arm to the shoulder laid bare,
    That the sinews may play in their might:
Let us strike for the manhood we feel within,
    And then we will strike for the right.

There is truth in the fables left by the Greek
    (What truth in these fables dwell!)
Of Hercules smiting the heads off the beast,
    And searing each place as they fell.
This is still, in this planet, wherever he tread,
    God's own given mission to man,
That he watch for error uprearing her head
    And strike wherever he can.

Then seize the sledge-hammer of mighty life,
    Let the clanging blows resound;
He strikes the swiftest and surest of all
    Who stands on no vantage-ground.
Let this earth of ours, then, from end to end,
    Be the anvil steady and strong
Whereon we beat, in the sight of the gods,
    The hundred heads of wrong.

What though others around thee may turn from the fight
    And chatter, a six-feet ape,
Heed them not, for they, too, stand on God's own earth,
    But keep true to thyself and thy shape.
Life is earnest only to earnest men,
    Sings the high pure Schiller, and so
Let them fashion the blocks of their own rough lives
    To the models they worship below.

But he who can feel lying warm at his heart
    The higher nature of man,
And can widen the link between us and the brute,
    Let him step to the front of the van.
We will follow him on like a leader of old,
    And echo his battle cry;
Make way for men that will work like men,
    Or, failing, man-like will die.

Yes—the fight will be long, and the heart will droop,
    For the ill will seem to win;
But look through the smoke to the goal ahead,
    And fall back on thy strength within.
Each point that you gain is a stair in your life
    To lift you nearer the throng
Who have fought and conquer'd, or hero-like died,
    With their hands at the throat of some wrong.

Then, brothers, bring into this great world's field
    Firm heart and sure foot for the strife:
No anvils are we for each fool to beat out,
    His ape-like system of life.
We strive for a higher standard than his,
    As we echo our battle cry—
" Here are men who will work at the tasks of men
    Or, failing, man-like will die!"

LEDGIE COOPER.

By the bend of the stream stood the house of old Ledgie Cooper, a worthy man, who about a hundred years ago here kept a school. Ledgie was one of the cottage patriarchs who was an honour to the Crawick. We well remember of seeing a very aged man, one of the little lairds of Crawick, who, when a boy, was one of Ledgie's scholars, and who used to relate some curious anecdotes of him. One was that the adversary attempted to prevent him from praying in the dark by pulling forcibly by his coat behind. This anecdote he one day related in the school when speaking to the children on the necessity of persevering in it; but they, not rightly apprehending the thing, and supposing that the enemy was at that moment standing at the back of their venerable teacher, rushed all and every one out of the school in the utmost trepidation, and would not return till they were persuaded by the old Laird of Orchard to accompany him back, when composure was restored, and the work of the school went on as usual.—"*Voice from the Desert,*" *by the late Dr Simpson of Sanquhar.*

AULD Ledgie Cooper cam' into the schule,
 But his face was wae to see;
A sad, sad look was upon his broo,
 An' a sad look in his e'e.

He sat for a moment deep, deep in thocht,
 Wi' his broo on the airm o' the chair;
Then he gaed to the door to cry in the weans
 That were rinnin' here an' there.

They heard his voice at the dookin' pool,
 Away doon the howms o' Craw'ck,
They ran thro' the fiel's wi' their breeks i' their han',
 An' their sarks half ow'r their back.

They heard his voice in the Knockinhair Wood,
 They lookit roun' an' roun'—
"Is the schule in already?" they ask'd, an' flung
 The bluidy fingers doon.

They heard it up in the Orchard burn
　　As far as the deil's big stane;
They left tryin' to rub oot the pedlar's bluid,
　　An' cam' in ane by ane.

But as sune as they saw the dominie's broo,
　　Their hearts laup wi' sudden dreid,
An' ilk ane slippit away to his seat,
　　An' never lifted his heid.

Then Ledgie rase up wi' a wild fear'd look,
　　To say the mornin' pray'r;
But first he lookit up to the roof,
　　An' then in below his chair.

An' aye as he pray'd that God micht keep
　　Himsel' an' the weans frae sin,
He jamp, as ane micht at the stang o' a bee,
　　An' lookit roun' ahin'.

O, weel micht the scholars glow'r, an' weel
　　Micht they look in ilk ither's face,
As if something uncanny was in the schule,
　　Or was hingin' aboot the place.

But when Ledgie Cooper had finish'd the pray'r,
　　An' afore he turn'd to sit doon,
He dichted the sweat aff his broo, an' cried
　　At his scholars to gather roun'.

Ye scarce heard their feet as they cam' frae their seats,
　　Sic a fear was on them a';
But, when Ledgie sigh'd an' began to speak,
　　They scarce their breaths could draw.

"O, bairns, O, bairns," auld Ledgie began,
  "I got a fricht yestreen,
That made my heart loup up to my mouth,
  An' my hair stan' up like a preen.

Yestreen, as ye ken, was the Sabbath nicht,
  An' aye on that holy day
I read the Bible until it grows dark,
  An' then I kneel an' pray.

But my heart, last nicht, was an unco weicht,
  An' sairly bother'd wi' doot;
An' what gude cam' into my min' to say,
  My lips wadna let it oot.

For the deil himsel' cam' into my room,
  An' stood ahint my back;
An' a wauf o' his breath like a brimstone lowe
  Made my very han's grow black.

But I tried to pray as ane micht dae,
  Whase moments number'd be,
But he pu'd my coat tails, cryin', 'Ledgie, man,
  Pit in a word for me.'

Then I faun' his club fit stot against my ain,
  His han' slip alang my arm;
An' his touch was like to a reid-hot airn,
  For the place at ance grew warm.

Then I got a glint o' ane o' his horns
  Ow'r my shuider at the richt;
But I steekit my een, an' I hung my heid,
  To keep awa' that sicht.

An' I tried to pray, but nae word could I say,
    My tongue was as dry as could be,
For the deil was aye cryin', ' O, Ledgie, man,
    Will ye no speak a word for me?'

Then I faun' his tail creepin' roun' my waist,
    Wi' mony a twist an' turn,
An' I kent that his face was near to my ain,
    For my hair began to burn.

But I claspit my han's on my broo an' my een,
    As ye see me daein' the noo,
An' I tried to pray, till my throat grew dry,
    An' the sweat fell aff my broo.

But juist when the ane who hates us a'
    Began to pu' me away,
Like a sweet spring-well cam' the words to my mouth,
    An' I faun' that I could pray.

I pray'd fu' lood an' I pray'd fu' lang,
    Till I faun that I was free ;
But, alake ! dear weans, the fricht last nicht
    Has left queer thochts wi' me."

But what was Ledgie Cooper's surprise
    When he open'd up his een,
To see toom binks an' an open door,
    An' nae schule weans to be seen ?

For ilka ane at his frichtfu' tale
    Had saftly slippit away,
An' were rinnin' aboot like scatter'd sheep
    On the tap o' Carco brae.

Then, what wark had the laird o' Orchardburn
 An' Ledgie coaxin' them in;
But afore they could manage to catch them a'
 They had mony a weary rin.

Then Ledgie rase up when the door was shut,
 An' said, "O weans, what a fule
Was your maister to tell ye his fricht yestreen,
 That has made ye rin frae the schule.

But I only tauld it to teach you this,
 When ye a' grow up into prime,
That a body can stan' unco near the deil,
 If he's praying at the time."

IN THE VANGUARD.

INTO all the onward current and this iron time that feels
 Its own way with mighty clamour through this century of ours
Come I, while the toiling planet like some stricken monster reels
 In an overheat to reach the very climax of its powers.

But the ages ever watchful of their growing higher need,
 Cry—"Before we hail him poet, glowing with the vatic mood,
He must, with his brow turn'd upward, stand like rock upon his
  creed,
  Ours shall be the task to shelter what may spring from where he
   stood."

Then I answer—"One great creed is mine, but as the blinding sun
 Draws the unseen stars in day-time, though we try in vain to see,

So the lesser creeds twine round it, as it towers in height alone;
That one faith is trust in God and Christ and all the great To Be.

All the lesser are the social bands that knit me to my kind,
Further progress, higher culture, and the touch of purer thought,
Passing on the watchword 'Forward,' to another kindred mind,
Fighting for the broader platform as an earnest fighter ought."

Then the ages pause a moment, all unnoted of the earth,
Speak in earnest, half-heard whispers, then turn slowly round again,
Crying, "If this fellow yearns to battle for the purer birth,
Let him pass and fight it out amid his boasted fellow-men."

So I come, then, brothers, shoulder touching shoulder in the throng,
Shame if I could stand thus feeling all the kindred aims ye bear
With my lips shut, like Ridolpho's, as in Dante's solemn song,
Nor give one single echo to the music leaping there.

If there be in song a hidden, talismanic force and power,
That for ever lifts us upward to the purer life and thought,
It were something but to leave behind, though dying in an hour,
Some stray note of music chording with the great world's, as it ought;

Or, to think that in our toiling some quick fragment of that flame
Which from nature, Laocoön-like, clasps its coils of fire round men,
Might be put in words by us and shot, with hundred-tongued acclaim,
From firm heart to heart, until it struck back on our own again.

Ay, to catch in some wild frenzy, as the painter dash'd his brush
'Gainst the passive canvas, mad to grasp the wild wave's mimic foam,

All the thought that, like a Pallas, still unseen will ever rush
   From the brain of the wide present to the grander time to come.

So the deep, forecasting poet, glowing with his rhythmic art,
   Leans against the broad-based future while his soul in visions dips;
Rising with some mighty lyric, shooting throbs from heart to heart,
   Caught when nature fell upon him with her own apocalypse.

But I come not with such lyrics—mine have not the ring and sound
   To catch the swift world's straining ear, athirst for nobler things;
Yet my hand and heart are yearning for a power to be unbound,
   That my soul may catch some music worthy of the higher strings.

"Lo, he comes," perchance some whisper, "with a thought laid out
     for wrong,
   Little points of poison-blisters, plentiful in modern days;
Lo, he comes with something in him that unwisely takes to song,
   Croaking from a dusty railway for a paltry boon of praise!"

Heavens! praise were worthless fruit to pluck and gather in these
     years,
   When the loftier thought must grow, and all the lower, baser aims
That fling roots down, like the banyan, must be torn up with our tears,
   That the future may not wear upon its brow a thousand shames.

What is all this earth around us but a place to wrestle in,
   Foot to foot and hand to hand with all the beasts that must be
     fought?
Fight it out, and let the still gods turn their thumbs up when we win,
   Like the Romans in the circus when their blood ran swift and hot.

Fight with hate and scorn and envy, fight with all that saps the man;
   We have grand, true types before us, shame on those who turn
     and yield!

Better lying dead, to serve as stepping-stones to raise the van,
Than lose all this noble manhood, and return without our shield.

Oh, that some great painter, glowing with the secret of his art,
Would place upon the canvas, when his thought was pure and high,
A dead Spartan, killed in fight, that we might catch with soul and heart
The wild energy of purpose not yet quench'd within his eye!

Honour to the great and noble on whatever ground they stand,
If they give us higher stand-points—for such office were they sent;
Honour to them, if we feel the strong grasp of an unseen hand
Leading us to what they fought for by the pathways that they went.

In these days they speak of missions; noblest of them all is this,
That we train our manhood upward, till the grand old Hebrew thrill,
Which, ere Adam lost his splendour, ran like bands of steel through his,
Lies like fire about our hearts, to keep our purpose earnest still.

For we are not as some preach, with faithless hands that beckon doubt,
Drops of life from godless matter struck by some stray random touch,
When the forces play'd at blind buff, but by God Himself shaped out—
Autographs of Him in flesh, yet all unworthy to be such.

Then we dare not but move upward, though we falter in our tread,
Though we feel around our limbs the paralysing coils of fear;
Lo! afar we hear brave whispers coming from the earnest dead,
As the old heroic voices sung with winds in Ossian's ear.

Up, then, to our life-long fight, and fling the gage of battle down,
Let the ages bear our word of rally onward far and quick;
Nobler usage of this manhood, from the king who wears a crown
　Down to our own selves, my brothers, working with the spade and pick!

WHERE I AM LYING NOW.

THE first sweet wind of the summer
　Is breathing upon my cheek,
And swaying the heads of the grasses
　That throb with a wish to speak.
The spray is upon the hawthorn,
　The leaf is out on the bough,
　　The light swift birds
　　Are singing sweet words
Where I am lying now.

My head is upon a primrose,
　My hand on a violet,
My foot has bent down a daisy—
　It is looking up at me yet.
Two butterflies—one like snow-drift,
　The other like blood, I trow—
　　Dip their fairy hues
　　In the earth's sweet dews,
Where I am lying now.

I turn away from the sunlight
　That is falling soft and rife,
And I hear the angels spreading
　The miraculous network of life.

And still, as their hands are plying,
 They murmur a tender vow—
  From heaven to earth
  It is one great birth—
 Where I am lying now.

O, dweller within the city,
 Come forth from its smoke and dust,
And, were it but one hour only,
 Clean thy soul from its growing rust.
Here stretch thyself on this couch of grass,
 With a hand upon thy brow,
  And take a part,
  With a poet's heart,
 In the dreams I am dreaming now.

ROCK HIM TILL HE GROWS A MANNIE.

CUDDLE doon an' sleep fu' soun',
 Mammy's bairnie saft an' cozie;
Pit ae han' my neck aroun',
 An' the ither in my bozie.
There, noo, sleep while mammy sings
 That bit sang, fu' lown an' cannie—
Hoo a fairy every nicht
 Rocks him till he grows a mannie.

Just when he begins to sleep,
 In she comes—that dumpy fairy—
Askin' wi' auld-fashion'd look,
 " Let me try the wean to carry !"

But I shake my heid an' say,
  "Mammy daurna trust her bairnie
Wi' a thing sae licht as you;
  First grow bigger an' she'll learn ye."

Then I draw the creddle near,
  Pit him in, while sweet an' simple,
She gets up upon the stule,
  An' raxes doon to kiss his dimple;
After this she starts an' sings,
  As she rocks an' swings the creddle,
Sic a sang, sae lown an' sweet,
  I daurna speak a word or meddle.

What that sang can mean ava,
  Dim an' riddle-like in seemin',
Nane kens but this bairnie here,
  For he smiles an' starts the dreamin'.
Then that fairy, keekin' ow'r,
  Seein' this, sings laigh an' cannie,
"Rock him saft, an' rock him aft,
  Till he grows a great big mannie."

Then her sang begins to turn
  Saft an' wae, as if entreatin';
Though I dinna ken a word,
  Yet I maist fa' to the greetin'.
But the weanie still smiles on,
  Liftin' up a wee fat han'ie,
Which the fairy kissin' cries,
  "Bairnie, sleep an' grow a mannie."

So he sleeps the hale nicht lang,
  Waukin' up fu' gleg an' smilin',

For he min's the fairy's sang,
    An' the dreams that cam' beguilin';
But the meanin' o' the sang
    That a carefu' mither misses,
This bit laddie winna tell,
    Though she gi'es him fifty kisses.

Ay, the sleep that comes when we
    Are weans, an' rockit by oor fairy,
Fa's upon us saft as dew
    Frae heaven's threshold high and airy:
Then we ken the mystic sang,
    An' the forms we see when dreamin';
Pity that we miss them a'
    When we grow to men and women.

THE OLD SCHOOL-HOUSE.

AH! often when coming from labour,
    When I hear the children play,
There rises within me a vision
    Of the school-house far away—

The old, dark, humble school-house,
    That stood by the little stream,
That babbled and splash'd in the sunshine,
    Or slipp'd into pools to dream.

And, again, as I think of my childhood,
    And its circle of sunny land,

Comes the wish to stand by that streamlet,
    As of old I used to stand—

Just to listen again to its murmurs,
    As I did in that early time,
When my life—before and behind me—
    Had the ring of a poet's rhyme:

Or to stand on the bridge with the children,
    And give one long, deep shout,
That might sweep from my bosom's chamber
    The dust of manhood out.

For I weary and fret at the knowledge
    This manhood has brought to me,
And forever look back with a longing
    To the glory that used to be.

But vain is that pent-up yearning,
    And wish for the summer gleam
That ran through my young existence,
    Like the plot through a fairy's dream.

It has sunk away as the sunshine
    May fade from the breast of a hill,
And the shadow that now is around me
    Is misty and drear and chill.

But still, when I come from my labour,
    If I hear the children play,
Then my heart goes back to the school-house
    And the village far away.

THE DEIL'S STANE.

"In the very centre of the deep gorge of this linn is an immense boulder, estimated at thirty tons weight. It is a mass of water-worn granite, probably from the Isle of Arran, as its granulated particles seem to be precisely of the same character of those that compose the granite of Goatfell. It must have been conveyed in the age of the northern drift, or dropped from the base of some massive iceberg as it sailed the waters that erst covered these heights. It is rounded like an egg, and has a belt of finer grain begirding its bulk like an iron hoop around a barrel."—*Simpson's "Voice from the Desert."* Such is the account given by the late Dr Simpson of Sanquhar; but in the neighbourhood the boulder in question is known by the dignified appellation of the "Deil's Stane." How it came to get such a title I have not been able to learn. Long ago, a pedlar was murdered near the spot for the sake of the petty wares he traded with among the hills. They still show you his blood in the channel of the Orchard burn, close to where the stone is lying. This, like all other blood shed in like circumstances, will not wash out. I have, in the following poem, with the license usually granted to rhymers, wandered from received tradition in order to "point a moral and adorn a tale."

"WHAUR hae ye been, my bonnie, bonnie bairns,
    Sae lang awa' frae me?
Come in, come in, for I'm weary to hae
    Wee Jeanie upon my knee.

I lookit lang doon the howms o' the Craw'ck,
    Where the fairies by munelicht play,
Then up to the daisies that grow sae white
    On the side o' the Carco brae.

For I thocht that ye micht be pooin' flooers,
    An' weavin' them into a croon
For wee Jeanie's heid; but I saw na ane,
    Though I lookit roun' an roun'."

"O, grannie, grannie, we werena there,
    Nor yet in the howms doon by;
For we sat by the edge o' the Orchard burn,
    An' we heard the cushie's cry.

Then we frichten'd the troots wi' oor wee white feet,
　As we paidled up the burn,
Till they splutter'd to win frae oor sicht in the broo,
　Wi' mony a jouk an' turn.

But at last we waded nae farrer up,
　But set wee Jeanie her lane,
Wi' a bunch o' primroses in her han',
　On the tap o' the deil's big stane."

"O, bairnies, bairnies, what is't ye say?
　An' what does your grannie hear?
What made ye gang up to the deil's big stane—
　That place sae dark an' drear?

Alake, alake, when the clock strikes twal,
　What soun's an' what sichts are there;
When the howlet flaps wi' an eerie cry,
　Through the woods o' Knockenhair!

Then chields that hae drucken baith lang an' late
　At their howfs in Sanquhar toon,
As they staucher by hear the paidlar's cry,
　An' the big stane rumblin' doon.

But here, as we're a' sittin' roun' the fire,
　An' wee Jeanie upon my knee,
I will tell ye the tale o' the paidlar's death,
　As my mither tauld it to me.

Wee Mungo Girr was an auld, auld man,
　Wi' a hump upon his back;
But fu' yauld was he at speelin' a brae
　To a herd's house wi' his pack.

For the clink o' siller put smiles on his face,
    An' a gleg look in his e'e;
But wae to the greed that brocht on his doom,
    An' the death he had to dree.

He keepit his purse in a stockin' fit—
    A purse fu' heavy an' lang;
An' ilka mornin' he counted it ow'r,
    For fear that it micht gang wrang.

An' aye as the shillin's play'd slip aff his loof,
    An' jingled into the lave,
He scartit his heid, an' he hotch'd an' lauch'd
    Till he scarce could weel behave.

O, bairnies, bairnies, the love o' gowd
    Turns into an awfu' sin,
For the heart grows hard, an' lies dead in the breast,
    Like the bouk o' my nieve o' whin.

An' we canna look straicht in oor neebor's face,
    For oor human love gets thrawn;
An' we canna look up to the sky abune,
    For oor heid is downward drawn.

Sae Mungo, the paidlar, gaed aye half boo'd,
    Comin' up or gaun doon a brae;
For the luve o' the siller he liket sae weel
    Was in him by nicht an' day.

An' weel could he manage to wheedle an' sell,
    To the lassies oot on the hill,
A brooch for their shawls, or a finger ring,
    That was gowd in their simple skill.

But alake for the greed that hung ow'r his heid
  To bring him meikle woe,
As a thunder cloud rests on the high Balc Hill,
  An' darkens the fields below.

But I'll tell ye the tale that my mither tauld,
  When I was a toddlin' wean;
It will mak' ye nae mair tak' the Orchard burn
  To sit on the deil's big stane.

Ae afternoon, as Mungo, half boo'd,
  Held alang steep Carco brae,
Croonin' into himsel', for his heart was glad
  Ow'r the bargains he'd made that day;

A' at ance, afore ever he kent, a han'
  Touch'd the hump that was on his back,
An', turnin' roun', no a yaird frae himsel'
  Was a man that was cled in black."

"O, Mungo, Mungo, pit doon yer pack,
  An' sell to me," said he,
"A necklace for ane o' the witches o' Craw'ck,
  Wha has dune gude wark for me."

Then the paidlar open'd his pack in a glint,
  An' oot wi' the wanted gear;
"A shillin's the price;" said the man in black—
  "O, Mungo, your shillin's here."

Then he slippit the shillin' into his han',
  An' steppit alang the brae;
But what made Mungo jump up an' dance,
  Like schule weans at their play?

THE DEIL'S STANE.

Ay, weel micht he jump like daft, for he saw
    A joyfu' sicht, I wis;
Instead o' the shillin' a guinea lay there,
    That by nae kent law was his.

Yet he row'd it up in a cloot by itsel',
    For fear it micht grow dim,
An' never let on to the neebors he met
    O' the luck that had fa'en to him.

The next time gangin' ow'r Carco hcicht,
    A han' was laid on his back,
An', lookin' aroun', no a yaird frae himsel'
    Was the same man cled in black.

Then the paidlar's heart sank doon like a stane
    As he thocht to himsel', nae doot,
He has come again to tak' back his ain,
    That I canna dae withoot.

But he juist said, " Mungo, come doon wi' your pack,
    An' sell me richt speedily
A necklace for ane o' the witches o' Craw'ck,
    Wha has dune gude wark for me."

Then Mungo, richt happy that this was a',
    Cam' oot wi' the wanted gear;
" A shillin's the price;" said the man in black—
    "O, Mungo, your shillin's here."

Then he slippit the shillin' into his loof,
    While the paidlar steekit his een;
Nor open'd them up till the man in black
    Was naewhere to be seen.

Then he keekit into his loof, an' there
　　Lay anither gowd guinea bricht;
Sae he row'd it up wi' the first in a cloot,
　　An' thocht that a' was richt.

The next time gangin' ow'r Carco hill,
　　A han' was laid on his back,
An', lookin roun', no a yaird frae himsel'
　　Was the same man cled in black.

But a frichtfu' look was upon his broo,
　　As he leant against a stane
That Mungo had never seen there afore,
　　An' thirty tons if ane.

A fear lay cauld at the paidlar's heart,
　　As he sank doon on his knee—
"Come ye here to work me scaith or ill,
　　Or to buy a necklace frae me?"

The froon grew black on the stranger's broo
　　As he cried, like a thunder-peal,
"A necklace o' fire for the neck o' him
　　Wha cheats baith man an' deil."

Then the lowe cam' oot at his mooth an' een,
　　On ilk side o' his heid grew a horn,
As he seized the paidlar an' whirl'd him ow'r
　　The hill wi' a lauch o' scorn.

Doon, doon the hill, as ye ca' a gird,
　　Gaed Mungo, flung by the deil;
An' doon row'd that big stane after him,
　　As steady as some mill-wheel.

Then, keep us a'! what a soun' cam' up
    Wi' the paidlar's deein' cry;
It gaed doon the Craw'ck an' doon the Nith,
    An' awa' ow'r the hills oot by.

The big stane fell in the Orchard burn,
    It lies there till this day;
An' still at its fit is the paidlar's bluid,
    That winna wash away.

O, bairnies, bairnies, when ye grow up
    To be lads an' lasses fair,
Keep min' o' the death o' Mungo Girr,
    An' aye deal frank an' fair.

An', bairnies, be sure an' keep this in min',
    For I canna lang be here,
That the deil's big stane is on ilka ane's back
    Wha has love for nocht but gear.

THE FIRST-FOOT.

BRIGHT the firelight touch'd his portrait hanging on our humble
    wall,
But a sweeter light was in us, with a deeper, purer glow—
He was coming home, our darling—fair and frank, and broad and
    tall—
    First-foot on our simple threshold, cover'd with the New Year's
    snow.

"Twelve o'clock will strike, dear wife, before the train comes in
    to-night,"
Said my husband at the doorway, he, too, glad at heart and gay;
And he turn'd a step to meet me as I whisper'd, soft and light,
    " Let him enter first," and, smiling at my words, he went away.

Then I turn'd, my own heart bursting at the joy about to come,
    Drew the chair a little nearer to the glowing evening fire ;
Heard in freaks of my own fancy all the laughter and the hum
    Of a well-known voice that whisper'd ever at my least desire.

Fondly to myself I pictured all his much-prized honours won,
    Earnest of the future harvests that the years would open up ;
Caught a hundred whispers rising with this burden still "our son;"
    O ! a mother's joy has not one drop of gall within the cup.

Then I went, and by the window watch'd with eager gazing eye
    All the distant railway lights that slowly came in sight to me ;
Question'd to myself, "Now, which of these far lights is bringing
    nigh
Our first-foot for the New Year that in one little hour will be ?"

But a deep chill, like a viper's touch, crept through me as I stood,
    Bringing hand-in-hand a terror, as behind the furthest light
Rose another in the darkness, that, like one great splash of blood,
    Gleam'd like a murder seen of God within the folds of night.

Rooted to the place I stood, and watch'd its steady, fiery gleam,
    All the pulses in my being beating as in act to fail ;
And my heart sank down within me, like a stone flung in the stream,
    As behind it rose an engine's whistle with a ghostly wail.

For at that drear whistle all the years broke from their rusty bands,
    Each one teeming with its fatal slip that happen'd in a breath—

How a traitor wheel, or pointsman's hasty clutch of faithless hands,
Scatter'd broadcast twenty lives to grace the silent feast of death.

Ah! what battles hope had all that weary hour with countless fears;
What deep, silent prayers rose upward that the lips still fail'd to speak;
What deep pain within the bosom, with its load of unwept tears,
That would not give one kindly drop to soften brow and cheek.

Came the hour at last, and striking, each stroke sounded like a knell,
Bodeful of some fate—but, hark! a sound of footsteps at the gate;
And my tears burst from their prison, and rose upward like a well,
At the coming joy about to crown my long and weary wait.

Then I heard the sound of whispers faint, as if in awe suppress'd,
And with all my wild, deep dread within, I open'd up the door—
Saw a burden in strange arms, and in their silence found the rest—
O, my God! first-foot in heaven! and for days I knew no more.

Slowly dawn'd the truth upon me, as my life came back again—
How a signal, clear a moment to the engine-driver's eye,
Brought him on with ringing rush and crash against and through the train!
And my life's one hope lay mangled in that sudden shock and cry!

Years have pass'd, but still that time brings round the great red light to me;
With it come the solemn footsteps, and the whispers hush'd and low;
And again the door is open'd, while like one struck dumb, I see
My darling's blood with that round light upon the ghastly snow.

THE NEW YEAR.

FROM the dim, dread veil that in wisdom is cast
    Between men and the shadowy scope
Of the future, the young Year comes at last
    In the flush of his strength and hope.

And as onward he comes, firm of heart and tread,
    The ghosts of the vanish'd years
Place their long, thin hands as they bless on his head,
    While their eyes fill up with tears.

But a sadder look is on brow and cheek
    As he bends by the dying year,
To catch the word he in turn must speak
    In the world's toil-deafen'd ear.

Then the pale, hush'd years slowly gather round,
    With an anxious look in their eyes,
As they bend in their haste to hear the sound
    Of the word ere the old year dies.

And, lo! in a silence, as if of death,
    That word is given, and then
The ghosts of the years fade away like a breath,
    While the New comes forth to men.

And, hark! how the bells ring forth their mirth
    In the cool, still air above!
Oh, well may they peal to the ends of the earth,
    For the watchword whisper'd was " LOVE."

Then, brothers, here, ere our footsteps part,
    And we turn to our labour again,
Let that watchword still have a place in our heart
    As we toil amid toiling men.

So that we, too, dying, may leave behind,
    Ere the other shadows begin,
The same warm word in the hearts of our kind,
    Till the last New Year comes in.

BEHIND TIME.

"MORE coal, Bill," he said, and he held his watch to the light of
    the glowing fire;
" We are now an hour and a-half behind time, and I know that
    my four months' wife
Will be waiting for me at the doorway just now, with never a wish
    to tire;
But she soon will get used to this sort of thing in an engine-
    driver's life."

He open'd the furnace door as he spoke, while I, turning with
    shovel in hand,
Knock'd the fuel into the greedy flame, that was tossing and
    writhing about,
Leaping up from its prison, as if in a wrath it had not the power to
    command,
Shooting narrow pathways of sudden light through the inky dark-
    ness without.

Then I turn'd to my place, and as onward we clank'd I sang to
    myself a snatch
  Of a song, to keep time to the grinding wheel (my voice was as
    rough as its own);
While Harry cried over, from time to time, as he stole a look at
    his watch,
  "Making up for our little delays now, Bill, we shall soon catch
    the lights of the town."

A steady fellow was Harry, my mate, with a temper like that of a
    child;
  Loved by all on the line.—"Keeps time like Harry," the guards
    used to say.
What a marriage was that of his when it came, and how we stokers
    went wild
  To deck our engines with ivy and flowers in honour of such a day.

A nice happy maiden he got for a wife, but a little timid, poor
    thing—
  Never could rest when her husband was late, our "pitch-ins" were
    getting so rife;
And this would make Harry cry over to me, as we thunder'd with
    rush and swing,
  "Always like to run sharp to time for the sake of my little wife."

We were now dashing on at a headlong speed, like the sweep of a
    winter wind,
  When a head-light in front made me step to his side and cry,
    with my mouth to his ear—
"Joe Smith coming on with the midnight goods—he, too, is an
    hour behind;
  He should have been safe through Hinchley cutting, instead of
    passing us here."

On came the train; but ere we had reach'd in passing the middle part,
A heavy beam in one of the trucks, that had jolted loose from its place,
Crash'd through the storm-board, swift as a bolt, striking Harry full in the heart,
And sent him into the tender with death lying white on his manly face.

With a cry of horror I knelt by his side, and, lifting a little his head,
I saw his lips move as if wishing to speak, but the words were lost in a moan.
Harry! He open'd his eyes for a moment, then lifting his finger, said—
"O, Bill, my wife—behind time;" and I was left on the engine alone.

My God! what a journey was that through the night, with the pall-like darkness before,
And behind the dead form of my mate muffled up, looking ghastly, rigid, and dumb;
And ever on either side as I turn'd, a face at a half-shut door
Peering into the street, to listen the sound of footsteps that never would come.

How that frail slight wife bore the terrible death of the one she had loved so well
I know not; the horror of that one night with the dead was enough to bear;
And the guardsmen who bore their sad burden home, had not language left them to tell
Of the awful depths to which sorrow will reach when led by a woman's despair.

Ah! years have gone by since then, but still when I hear the
  guards say, " Behind time,"
Like a flash I go back to that hour in the night, mark'd red in
  my life's return sheet,
And again in my terror I kneel by Harry, struck down in his manly
  prime,
While his four months' wife stood waiting to hear the wish'd-for
  sound of his feet.

A WALK TO PAMPHY LINNS.

<small>The following poem was the result of a visit which I, along with three others, paid to Pamphy linns, a romantic spot lying hidden in a wood which stretches along the Barr Moor in the neighbourhood of Sanquhar. I have availed myself of a poetical license, and described the linns as swollen by rains, and foaming down the waterfall which forms the *pièce de resistance* of the place. The friends who accompanied me will pardon me where I have deviated from fact to fiction, especially my young Edinburgh friend whom I have bored in the text. The poem is warmly dedicated to the three.</small>

WE took a walk to Pamphy linns—
  Three other friends and I,
Glad-hearted as when day begins
  With summer in the sky.

Our talk was edged with homely wit,
  The banter flew apace,
And ever at a happy hit
  The laughter clad our face.

But we were used to each, and knew
  The harmless fence of tongue;
So quip and jest rose up and flew
  And prick'd, but never stung.

The lark was far above our head,
    The daisy at our feet,
The heather show'd a coming red
    Of tiny blossom sweet.

The sheep turn'd round to see us pass,
    The milky snow-white lambs
Gamboll'd and sniff'd the growing grass,
    Or nestled by their dams.

The pure air brought the far hills near,
    Their furrows came to sight;
And here and there a stream grew clear,
    And smiled in the sunlight.

" O, friend of mine, who late," I said,
    " Has left the streets of men,
Let all this quiet overhead
    Bring back thine own again.

Look how the Earth puts forth her pride
    And blooms around, to draw
Thy soul out till it toss aside
    The phrases of the law.

For what are musty words to this—
    Your writs and *pros* and *cons*—
When Nature, full of summer bliss,
    Her summer vesture dons ?

So, Faust-like, own her quiet power,
    And let her have her will,
And let thy fingers clasp a flower,
    Instead of inky quill."

Our path lay through the sunny fields,
   In gentle ups and downs;
Dear heart! I thought, but nature yields
   A bliss unmatch'd in towns.

At length we reach'd a shepherd's cot,
   That sat between two woods—
Fit home for all the stirless thought
   That, dove-like, sits and broods.

I knew the shepherd; for a space
   We rested by his hearth,
And saw the moorland on his face,
   And in his honest mirth.

O! blessings on a hillside life
   That trammels not the heart,
But in its gentle pleasures rife
   Stands with its back to art.

How far above the studied speech
   Of empty polish'd sound,
That glides within a proper reach,
   Where rule has set the bound.

And blessings on the girl who stood
   In better garb than silk,
And proffer'd to us, shy of mood,
   A glass of cooling milk.

Her cheek was soft with health's fair tint,
   And in her drooping eye
Sweet thoughts came up that fain would hint
   That maidenhood was nigh.

Her brow was open, frank, and free,
    Half-hid by wealth of tress—
A very Wordsworth's girl was she
    For woodland simpleness.

So, Janet, half-way through thy teens,
    And all the world to learn,
Lean to thine own sweet heart, as leans
    From moss-clad rock the fern :

And hear the wish that springs from mine
    Before I pass away—
Keep thou that simple life of thine,
    Take to the town who may.

We reach'd a belt of wood at last,
    And with a lusty cheer
I cried, " Now all our toil is past,
    For Pamphy linns are here."

We took the shaded path that led
    To the turf-clad foot-bridge,
Then struck into the streamlet's bed,
    And held along its edge.

We reach'd the falls, and, looking round,
    On either side were trees,
And at our feet the hurrying sound
    Of water ill at ease.

Huge rocks with moss half-cover'd dipt
    Or in the stream reclined,
As if they once had partly stript
    To bathe, but changed their mind.

O'er these the water foam'd and splash'd
    In many a whirl and turn,
Or from moss'd outlets peep'd and dash'd
    To kiss a wander'd fern.

We clomb the highest peak of rock,
    And, halting there to breathe,
Heard with continual splash and shock
    The water run beneath.

Then, rising, down the fretted steep
    To reach the base below
We struggled, careful heed to keep,
    As Alpine hunters go.

We reach'd the foot, and found a rest
    Beneath the trees' sweet shade,
Where Nature for her woodland guest
    A flower-deck'd seat had made.

From there we watch'd the falls above,
    The rocks half-worn and gray,
That still, like shapeless Sphinxes, strove
    To tear their veils of spray.

A dreamy, cooling murmur went,
    Like winds when spring is near,
Through all the trees, that stood intent,
    And prick'd their leaves to hear.

I leant back in a shady place,
    Where sunlight could not gleam :
If poets are a dreaming race,
    Then here they well might dream.

But "Further down" was still the cry—
"Down to the seat," they said;
"There let another hour go by—
The hanging rocks o'erhead."

So there we went, and with our knives
We roughly carved our names,
As some carve out their shorten'd lives
With vacillating aims.

And as I carv'd, a primrose bright
Look'd on with wondrous eye,
As if for ever in its sight
A troop of fays pass'd by.

Upon the rocks, from German rhyme,
I writ two lines to say—
"O, happy time of love's young prime,
Would it could last alway."*

But ere we turn'd our path to trace,
I cried, "Farewell, thou stream!
If poets are a dreaming race,
Then here they well might dream."

So through the woods we went, but still
What German Schiller sung
Came ever up against my will,
And somewhat lightly stung.

O, happy time when love is sweet,
And life takes little heed,

* "O, das sie ewig grünen bliebe,
Die schöne zeit der yungen liebe."—*Das lied von der Glocke.*

But rolls a rainbow at our feet,
  Would it could last indeed!

And every flower in shaded nook,
  Speedwell and violet,
Cried, with a wonder in their look—
  So big, and dreaming yet?

Then out at last into the fields,
  Tinged with the daisy's dyes;
Dear heart! I said, but nature yields
  A bliss the town denies.

O fair is Edina, I said,
  And took my young friend's arm,
For there the magic past hath shed
  An ever-growing charm.

Twice have I trod its streets, and heard
  In fancy all the while
Legends in hints and whisper'd word
  From narrow street and pile.

But still the eye from every quest
  Would stop, to wander on
To those gray rocks that had for crest
  The lordly pile of stone.

Up, up it tower'd, as if in rage
  The modern change to view;
Like Carlyle, from the middle age,
  With brow knit at the new.

I, too, have touch'd Queen Mary's robe,
  With well-shaped Darnley nigh;
Have heard the murder'd Rizzio sob
  With blood-choked, helpless cry.

While through this war of uncheck'd will,
  Its battles, broils, and shocks,
A stirring voice was speaking still—
  The voice of fearless Knox.

God! when upon his grave I stood—
  Now daily trod by feet—
His soul went flashing through my blood
  In mighty waves of heat.

For great, good men can never die,
  Howbeit the ages roll;
But still unseen are ever nigh,
  To strengthen soul by soul.

But past is all that reign of force,
  Its deeds of blood and pain,
Gone as a river dries its source,
  Never to fill again.

For lo! to hide each bloody spot
  A nobler comes behind;
The curbless sway of growing thought,
  The dynasty of mind:

Which changes, and hath changed the earth,
  As gods the sculptor's stone;
A universal Protean birth,
  Whose *fiat* thunders on.

There, too, beneath the statued dome
    He sits, the Scott we claim;
Fit Mahomet for those who come
    As pilgrims of his fame.

Light was his task, some cry, but he,
    He changed the novel's bent;
And with its Gothic tracery
    A chaster purpose blent.

I pass those mighty ones, who then
    Were ever in my sight—
Strong kings who struggled with the pen
    To widen human right.

Yes! Edina is fair, and sweet
    This summer day would be
If I could lie on Arthur's Seat,
    And my schoolmate with me.

For still her magic power prevails,
    And still my thoughts take wing
To her, the city of the tales,
    Without its roving king.

But shame on me that I should prate
    Of all that city's grace
And beauty in such quiet state
    Around my own sweet place.

For look! three miles adown the vale
    Sanquhar lies in gray light;
And further on, time-struck and frail,
    The castle lifts its height.

Bones of the iron age, it stands,
    And, as to madness grown,
Flings down each year, from powerless hands,
    A crutch of scatter'd stone.

And right before us, near yet far,
    Furrow'd with winter rills,
That dry in summer like some scar,
    Stretch out the Todholes hills.

And speck-like at their base is seen
    The cot of shepherd Dryfe—
True soul of honest heart and mien,
    And simple mountain life.

But here is Killo bridge, and there
    Nestles old Killoside;
My blessings on the homely pair
    Who 'neath its roof abide.

And right in line that puff of smoke
    That every moment comes,
Is Bankhead, where, in ceaseless yoke,
    The engine clanks and hums.

A little further on we pace,
    Then through a field again,
And all at once, before our face,
    Kirkconnel full and plain.

I see the churchyard and the church,
    The gravestones standing by;
You need not through our Scotland search
    For sweeter place to lie.

And further up I catch the gleam
    Upon the pastor's pool;
The manse above, still as a dream,
    Stands in the shadows cool.

But there, from schoolhouse to the mill,
    Our hamlet stretches out;
Without one stir it slumbers still,
    Save when the schoolboys shout.

And now we cross the new foot-bridge,
    And shun the stepping-stones;
Nor loiter to lean o'er the edge
    To hearken Nith's sweet tones;

But hasten on, when just behind
    That line of thatch and slate,
An express train tears like the wind,
    And twenty minutes late.

THE VEILED MEMNON.

A FLUSH from the far land of song he came.
    To us;
His harp was strung with fiery threads of flame,
    That made his very music luminous.

He touch'd its strings, and as he softly sung,
    His eye
Had the divine intelligence that flung
    An awe on those who saw it passing by.

His brow was a fit palace for high thoughts,
  And far
Visions of splendour, as through cave-like grots
 When the sun flashes through them, with no bar

To stop the shafts of light. Upon his lips
  There lay
The tremulous feelings, as when sunshine dips
 Within the stream that smiles and slips away.

He stood Apollo-like, and grasp'd his song,
  Which wore
The impetuous thunder flashing full on wrong,
 And lurid lightnings that in swiftness bore

Heaven's message to the earth-dried hearts of men,
  Who felt
A new life stirring in them, which again
 Around it other higher wisdom dealt.

The deep oracular abyss wherein
  Is laid
Truth, with her million bolts that lie within,
 Forged on the anvils of the years, and made

Proof to the rust of time, were his to wield.
  He flung
Their sharp keen points with God's own signet seal'd,
 While the world's confines with their echoes rung.

Men came around him, hailing him as one
  Who saw
The clearer uplands of this life, that shun
 The nether mist. His word was as a law

Binding them to the right.   As priests of old
  Gave out
The oracular answers of their gods to hold
 The people to their faith.   So without doubt

They heard him; for his music, wing'd with fire,
  Flew up,
Waving on either side, as in desire
 For the far blue of skies.   As from a cup

We take the water, so they took his song;
  They hail'd
Him as a prophet doing war with wrong—
 His voice went everywhere, and still prevail'd.

But as he shaped his song, upon his eyes
  And lips
A shadow fell, from out the nether skies,
 Which gave birth unto dread; as a fear clips

Footholds for doubt to climb, so those who saw
  The change
Began to question, with wild looks of awe,
 As the high melody took lower range,

Striking base notes to tickle brutish ears:
  Is this
The old music which we held as from the spheres,
 Whose harmony was like a flood of bliss,

Drenching our being with a pure delight,
  As dew
Drenches the many-colour'd flowers when night
 Retires, and all the stars grow dim to view?

THE VEILED MEMNON.

He has but fool'd us, singing as in scorn
    That we
Should lift ourselves so high up, but to mourn
  The unattainable we cannot see,

Or reach! If God had touch'd him with the touch
    And strength
To make us better—we had need of such—
  To draw us onward—but to turn at length

And blend the poet's holocaustic fire,
    Which burns
The earth-growth from the spiritual desire,
  With all the lower life that ever spurns

The high pure thought, to wallow in low need,
    Were deep
Unutterable shame, to make him bleed
  And moan forever in his soul's wild sleep.

But we have lost him. Henceforth unto us
    He stands
A veilèd Memnon, no more luminous;
  The purer harp-strings broken in his hands:

Snapp'd as in wrath that they should echo tones
    Unmeet
To catch the ear, even in wailing moans
  For all the change that quench'd their fire and heat.

Shelley kept his wild music wondrous clear;
    He bent
His soul in flights of melody, which here
  Are with us still, and speaking, as if lent

For an eternity.   And others who
          Became
Singers have kept their music firm and true
   To God's first purpose, singing without shame,

Because they felt their mission.   In their band
          Is all
The splendour and the fire which, as they stand
   Shines on them, as a flood of sunbeams fall

Upon some distant hill.   Theirs be the meed
          Which song
Gives unto those who wrestle on with deed,
   And high endeavour for the end of wrong.

But his!   Hereafter when we name his name
          And powers
Shall we blush, owning him in very shame
   That he was one whose music was not ours?

Well! we have still his early music yet,
          The worst
Which follow'd after we can now forget
   In the impulses given by the first.

Enough!   God knows the time to lift His hand
          And take
The veil from off the Memnon, and command
   The music to turn purer for His sake.

THE CUCKOO.

*"Der kukuk ruft —
Wenn mit Blumen die Erde sich kleidet neu."—Schiller.*

AMID the sound of picks to-day,
   And shovels rasping on the rail,
A sweet voice came from far away,
   From out a gladly greening vale.

My mate look'd up in some surprise;
   I half stopp'd humming idle rhyme;
Then said, the moisture in my eyes,
   "The cuckoo, Jack, for the first time."

How sweet he sung; I could have stood
   For hours, and heard that simple strain;
An early gladness throng'd my blood,
   And brought my boyhood back again.

The primrose took a deeper hue,
   The dewy grass a greener look;
The violet wore a deeper blue,
   A lighter music led the brook.

Each thing to its own depth was stirr'd,
   Leaf, flower, and heaven's moving cloud,
As still he piped, that stranger bird,
   His mellow May-song clear and loud.

THE CUCKOO.

Would I could see him as he sings,
    When, as if thought and act were one,
He came; the gray on neck and wings
    Turn'd white against the happy sun.

I knew his well-known sober flight
    That boyhood made so dear to me;
And, blessings on him! he stopp'd in sight,
    And sang where I could hear and see.

Two simple notes were all he sung,
    And yet my manhood fled away;
Dear God! The earth is always young,
    And I am young with it to-day.

A wondrous realm of early joy
    Grew all around as I became
Among my mates a bearded boy,
    That could have wept but for the shame.

For all my purer life, now dead,
    Rose up, fair-fashion'd, at the call
Of that gray bird, whose voice had shed
    The charm of boyhood over all.

O! early hopes and sweet spring tears,
    That heart has never known its prime
That stands without a tear and hears
    The cuckoo's voice for the first time.

THE LOST EDEN FOUND AGAIN.

THE angels look'd up into God's own eyes,
As He shut the gateways of Paradise;

For they heard coming up from the earth below
A wail as of mortals in deepest woe;

And bending their far keen vision down,
Saw two on the earth from whom hope had flown.

Then the foremost one of the angels said,
Drooping his wings and bowing his head—

"Here, Father, are two in Thy shape and ours
Who have lost the light of their bridal bowers,

And wander, blind in their tears, and tost
With the thoughts of their Eden for ever lost."

Then God said, turning His face on him—
"Look once again, for thine eyes are dim."

Then the angel look'd, and, lo! he could see
A smiling babe on the woman's knee.

While the man bent down, and within his eyes
Was the light of his former Paradise.

Then the angel whisper'd—"My fears were vain,
For man has found his lost Eden again."

IN ROME.

A POEM IN SONNETS

"Roma! Roma! Roma!
Non è piu come era prima!"

I.

TO-MORROW I will be in Rome, and thou
   Within thy village. I can see thee stand,
Thine eyes in the direction of this land:
Fair pillar of the past, as it is now
The refuge of its heirlooms. In my ears
   I hear thee speaking as upon that day
   We parted, saying—"When thou goest away
To make a golden epoch in thy years
By travel, speak not of the Rhine's broad roll,
   Mount Blanc, the Yungfrau, or the Alps that rise
   Like icy Titans, nor of sunset skies;
But when thou come'st to Rome let all thy soul
   Fly to the past, and as it speaks to thee
   From out its temples, speak thou so to me."

II.

The one dream of our boyhood! Dost thou not
   Remember how we stood in mimic fight,
And marshall'd all our legion's puny might,
Then fann'd ourselves to ardour fierce and hot?
"Thus struck a Roman for his Rome!" we cried—
"Thus, thus into the gulf a Curtius leapt!"
And with a sudden shout and rush we swept
The foe back, till they fled on every side.
Then came the hymn of triumph, and the car
   Bearing the victor to the feast and wine,
And the delights of smiling peace and home;
   All this was with me of that mimic war,
As I passed through the arch of Constantine,
And stood within the centuries and Rome!

III.

If thou have, for the weak, defenceless past
   Aught in thee like to reverence, be dumb,
   And speak not, but let thought and feeling come
As mourners, and in kindred silence cast
Their sorrow on this city, now no more
   The foreground of the world, but lying dead,
   While the great present with its hasty tread
Moves on, and turns not save but to deplore.
The background of our Planet! But in death
   She hath that awe which broods upon the face
   Of the new dead, so in her fallen place
A power is with her still, though all her faith
   Is snapt like her own temples in the dust,
   And fades with centuries of age and rust.

IV.

I am in Rome, and underneath the spell
   Of her past glory; as I tread her streets,
   My soul keeps saying, as a child repeats
Its lesson—"The Eternal, here they dwell!"
I am alone, though in the busy crowd,
   Yet mighty spirits keep their pace with mine:
   Horace and Virgil, and those names divine
That in the world for ever speak aloud.
The past is with me, and my eyes are blind
   To all the modern change on either side;
   I stride a Roman, with a Roman's stride,
And feel a Roman's firmness fire my mind.
   I even hail the victor from afar,
   And join the throng that shout behind his car.

V.

Yet after all, when the soul finds its home,
   And we look with our daily eyes, we ask
   (Doubt round us like a mist) "Can this be Rome?"
And the slow answer is a mighty task.
Can this indeed be Rome, who from her heart
   Sent shocks of life, like blood, through distant lands,.
   Whose Kings were sons to her by Roman bands
Of valour, and their tribute fill'd her mart?
The Jupiter of cities! Now, alas!
   Upon her throne of seven hills, she seems
   The shadow of a thousand former dreams,
Pointing to all the splendid pomp that was.
   Even her columns seem to start and glow
   Into Cassandras, and wail forth her woe.

VI.

Where'er thou stand in ancient Rome there seems
   A shadow with thee ; and if thy keen thought
Turn pilgrim to the shrine of thy great dreams—
   Paying continual homage as it ought—
Thou art but fool'd ; and if thou rear again
   Columns and gods and temples, and within
The silent Forum place her mightiest men,
   Whose eloquence could calm and still the din
Of factions, lo ! the Presence at thy side
   Cries, "*Siste, viator,*" and from out the past
Thy soul comes, and instead of all the pride
   And high magnificence that was, thou hast,
Like garments of the mighty flung away,
Marbles and columns in one mix'd decay.

VII.

What high, great thoughts might leap within the breast
   Of the stern Romulus, that day when he
Ran a light furrow round his Rome to be,
Built huts, and, for a moment, took his rest.
Would he had been a Capys then, and seen,
   From the rude doorway, all the splendid power
   Taking still birth from out that quiet hour,
And spreading like a shadow all between
The earth and sky, until its mighty wings
   Were at full stretch, and a great empire stood
Flinging steel network over earthly things,
   Till, tired of uncheck'd force and constant blood,
Turn'd like the Titans, when it thus had striven,
And dared to parcel out the rights of heaven.

VIII.

I saw the mighty form of giant Time !
   He stood; within his hands were balances:
   He held them up; two kingdoms were in these;
One sunk; the other rose and flower'd to prime.
Around his feet his sons, the young, keen years,
   Wrestled and shaped fresh worlds; as they shaped
   They look'd up; through their lips a moan escaped,
And in their eyes was something like to tears.
Then with one voice they cried—" Is not the hour
   Ready ? Put down thy balances, and lift
   The nations we have foster'd as a gift
For thee." And Time, frowning till eyebrows met,
   Shook his white locks in sternly potent power,
Then whisper'd back to them—" Not yet, not yet !"

IX.

St Peter's ! how thy soul within thee grows
   And widens out in worship, as if God
   Had made this dome a moment His abode;
Then left His awful shadow to repose
Within its walls for ages. Let no speech,
   Or aught of earth be with thee, in this hour
   When the full past falls, like a sudden shower
Upon thee, bringing into all thy reach
The sacredness of what it hallows, till
   Thou standest not on marble but on air,
Feeling thyself uplifted by the will
   Of some great Presence dwelling everywhere;
Then, looking up, see right before thine eyes
God's very threshold to the bending skies.

X.

The first brief hour within the Vatican
　Is one in which thy soul can find no speech ;
　But dumbly yearns to gain those points to which
Climb the great possibilities of man.
Frescoes, mosaics, statues ; all that speaks
　Of the creative and refining power—
　God's share in man—that ever like a dower
Falls on him, and in fruitful silence seeks
High forms to build it forth, is here ; and we,
　Who pilgrimage to all our greater kind,
Know not the force that leads us, but must bow
　Before the eternal Roman sway of mind,
Blind with the same clear light which now I see
　Upon the beautiful Meleager's brow.

XI.

To shape, when the pure thought was high and free,
　Some mighty god, that, ever as we look,
　We feel its godhead with a stern rebuke
Claim worship, and we almost bend the knee—
This is the task of those grand souls who stand
　A thousand years between them ; for the given
　Fire, burning at the very core of heaven,
Cannot be flung broadcast from out the hand ;
But where it lights, ay, there it ever burns,
　A clear flame on the ember'd hearth of Time,
Quenchless but with himself.　Lo ! how it turns
　From the high Greek and all his higher glow,
And, shooting onward to a sister clime,
　Crowns with no stint a later Angelo.

XII.

The thoughts that only mate with gods alone,
   And all that high conception when the mind
   Looks heavenward for a model to its kind
Of what a god may be, meet here in stone.
The Sun God! Dost thou not behold him now
   With head thrown back, as if his native sky
   Had come, in some wild moment, all too nigh,
Then fled, but left its splendours on his brow?
Thou glorious Archer! In that awful hour,
   Granted by heaven, did the sculptor kneel
Before his chisel touch'd the virgin block,
   Feeling thy presence give consent and power?
We know not. We can only see and feel
   That heaven's fire with his sped every stroke.

XIII.

Back to the grand Apollo! Tell me not
   A mortal had to do with this. I know
   That if a god content him here below,
A mightier god must bind him to the spot.
Can this be genius that can so enthral,
   And lift us, Mahomet-like, until we feel
   The very heaven around us, and we reel
In the delight of worship? Who can call
This splendid triumph stone? Say rather we
   Behold a god who came to men, and met
His punishment in marble; yet he lives
   While we, with all our throbbing being set,
Worship with the bold thought that it may be
   Idolatry that heaven itself forgives.

XIV.

I turn'd from the Apollo with my mind
  Back to the Venus. I can see her now
  Looking at me with that divine-like brow
Round which the adoring world will ever bind
Its love for ages. All that hath been sung
  Since time grew up to manhood lingers round
  That snowy form, that ever seems spell-bound
In its own whiteness, and for ever young.
We lose our being as we look and wear
  Into her beauty, and become as naught;
  We are the stone, and she the glowing thought,
Haunting us with her presence everywhere—
  Goddess of Love—and we who stand but seem
  To touch the confines of her endless dream!

XV.

I see her yet—the glorious shape to which
  The pilgrim fondly wanders! Let me kneel,
  As if in that one act my soul could feel
And, all miraculously lifted, reach
The sculptor's height in that impassioned hour
  When the fair dream the world will not let die
  Took shape in stone, as if a god were nigh,
Limb, breast, and brow asserting conscious power
And claiming worship. O! did she look thus
  In that sweet hour, when glowing from her flight
  She knelt by Endymion in delight,
Kissing his brow and lip, and tremulous
  With sighs from heaven, whisper, "It is he,
  The Latmian!"—and so let her passion free.

XVI.

I stood before the Laocoön, and felt
    A soul move in the stone; as if the pain
Forever prison'd there had power to melt
    And fuse itself in double strength again
Into the gazer as he stands, and feels
    The marble horror catch his breath until
He sinks, and, in his very weakness, reels
    Before that form those coilings never kill.
Look on the father who with quivering form
    Strives to unlace the strain that never slips,
But keeps eternal clasp upon the place;
    While all the agony, like a lake in storm,
Moves from huge limbs to straining finger tips,
    Then makes a dread Vesuvius of the face.

XVII.

Temple of all the gods! and here the dust
    Of one reposes, who with early fame
    Went into death, and left behind the name
Of Raphael, to defy the years' quick rust.
How shall we name him who with quick, pure eyes
    Saw Heaven's Divinest, and in earth-made hues
    Painted the glory of His look, as dews
Catch the first light that falls from summer skies?
Say, poet of Christ in colours, who stood near
    The light of heaven, until its very strength
    Took him all kindly to itself at length,
Yet left him not, but went before his bier,
    And, soul-like in that work,* his last and best,
    Saw the great Master enter into rest.

       * The Transfiguration.

XVIII.*

The stone rolls from His feet like mountain mist;
   Before Him, ghost-like, in the vanquish'd tomb,
   The bands of linen lie within the gloom—
White pledges of the newly-risen Christ.
He comes forth! from the splendour of His brow
   Gethsemane and the Cross have fled. He stands,
   A halo of love around Him, as His hands
Clasp each in prayer; God's early morning glow
   Falls on Him, matching in those deep, sad eyes
The light of conquest gain'd for all our race,
   As if God bent Himself, and from above
Shed on Him all the glory of the skies;
   While the earth, dumb at such astounding love,
Turns round to gaze forever on His face.

XIX.

Here on this spot the heroic martyr† stood,
   God's fire upon his brow and in his heart,
   As the two gladiators drew apart
Glaring at each in their wild thirst for blood.
Lo! as the centuries roll aside their gloom
   We see him yet; the hero as he sinks
   Keeps to his purpose born of Christ, nor shrinks
Though human tigers track him to his doom.
Talk of this planet's holy spots! my feet
   Within this amphitheatre are on
   Its holiest, for a brother here alone
Stood up for God and man, till in the heat
   Of Roman thirst for blood he sank, and pass'd
   An early Livingstone, but not the last.

---

* One of Raphael's pictures, unfortunately lost or destroyed, was the Resurrection of our Saviour, who is represented bursting out of the sepulchre, "perhaps," says the authoress of *Rome in the Nineteenth Century*, "one of the grandest conceptions in the world."

† Telemachus.

XX.

I saw the stage of Time, and on it kings
   Strutted and fought, then laid them on the bed
   Of earth, that took them, like the blood they shed,
Kindly; and they were with forgotten things.
Then nations rose, who, branching out, became
   The very backbone of the universe.
   They reach'd their bloom until, as when a curse
Withers, they shrank and dwindled like a flame
   That lacks fresh fuel. All this while I saw
   Shadows creep o'er their ruins, and in awe
I turn'd to Time, and ask'd him to define
   These shadows; and he answer'd thus to me—
   "These are the forecasts of great worlds to be;"
I woke, and I was on the Palatine.

XXI.

Are nations, then, like flowers that have their bloom,
   Dying, as the still centuries pass away?
Alas! behind their acmè lurks the doom
   To write its "Mene" on corroding clay.
Belief, whether it be in gods or God,
   Can still work miracles; but if it fail,
   And Argus doubt with poisonous darts assail
Its inmost hold; then realms and men corrode.
The centuries behind teach this. Look back!
   Lo! from the wreck of worlds stand Greece and Rome
As skeleton witnesses of this, whose track
   Shows what may be when doubt has found a home.
I stood in Rome, but, when this came to me,
My England! I was looking back to thee.

XXII.

Two of great England's singers, lying each
    By each : one rose up wroth at human wrong,
And hung half-way to heaven in his song,
Till the heart burst in his desire to teach
The melody he heard from where he was.
    The other wander'd to the early past
    Yearning with a boy's ardour to recast
Its mythologic utterances. But as
The sun takes dews, so did their beauty him ;
    He pass'd, leaving behind sweet words that must
Forever keep him here. The other, too,
    Left melody that still will float and swim ;
Aerial mist with heaven shining through,
    And here a foot or two divides their dust.

XXIII.

Cor Cordium, thou art near to Shelley's heart ;
    Stop, if thou canst, the beatings of thine own,
For here a purer beats a perfect part,
    And models thought upon a purer tone.
Ay, Shelley's heart, it may be naught to thee,
    But in it lay the light which, though unseen,
Had the full stamp of that which is to be—
    It now is, but the earth is all between.
I claim no tears for him. If thou art one
    Who hears between the breathing of the years,
Thou shalt not miss his music ; if alone,
    It shall be sweeter and seem from the spheres ;
For his was from the higher realm of good
Brought down to men, not to be understood.

XXIV.

And wilt thou go away from Rome, nor see
    The resting-place of Keats, from whom thy soul
    Took early draughts of worship and control—
Poet thyself, and from beyond the sea?
I turn'd, and stood beside his grassy grave,
    Almost within the shadow of the wall
    Honorian; and as kindred spirits call
Each unto each, my own rose up to crave
A moment's sweet renewal by the dust
    Of that high interchange in vanish'd time,
    When my young soul was reeling with his prime;
But now my manhood lay across that trust.
    Ah! had I stood here in my early years,
    This simple headstone had been wet with tears.

XXV.

I go, for wider is the space that lies
    Between the sleeper in this grave and me;
    I look back on my golden youth, but he
Cannot look backward with less passion'd eyes.
There is no change in him; the fading glory
    Of mighty Rome's long triumph is around,
    But cannot come anear or pierce the bound
Of this our laurell'd sleeper, whose pale story
Takes fresher lustre with the years that fly.
    But Roman dust upon an English heart
    Is naught, yet this is Keats's, and a part
Of England's spirit. With a weary sigh
    I turn from sacred ground, and all the way
    Two spirits were with me—Keats and David Gray.

XXVI.

I left the crowd to its own will, and mused
　　Upon thy village life, that scarcely opes
　　One pathway for the liberal thought, nor copes
With the result that broadens; but suffused
With straiten'd range of thought, keeps on, nor sees
　　The world with proper vision. Creeds and sects
　　Are here, still seeing within each defects,
And men will battle to the last for these.
It will be so. Yet think, ere we condemn,
　　What our faith is to us is theirs to them;
And so grow broad with sympathy, nor sink
　　Into the barren pasture of old saws,
　　But think that God will open up His laws,
And tell us we are safer than we think.

XXVII.

Tiber! thy city's great have sunk and died
　　Making her famous, yet thou rollest on
　　(For time shrinks back from nature); in thy tone
To me, a pilgrim standing by thy side,
A threnody comes forth and fills my ears;
　　And all the heroic annals of the past
　　Rise up, as if the hand of time had cast
Its fingers on the keyboard of the years,
Hymning their changes. What a mighty reach
　　From the wild, fierce, wolf-suckled twins until
Seven hills saw mighty Rome repose on each—
　　Gateway to worlds which she oped at will,
But now forever shut, and in her ken
No "sesame" to open them again!

XXVIII.

Tiber! before I pass away from thee,
    One other dream. I stand with half-shut eye,
    And hear a mighty army's vaunt and cry;
Then see within the pass the heroic Three.
Hark to the clang that strikes against the bridge
    That shakes (such strength was in a Roman's blow,
    When faith was potent centuries ago);
Then the loud crash, as two from off its ledge
Leap among friends. But where is he, the best,
    The mightiest—Horatius? In thy wave
    He plunges, and around him thou dost lave
Thy yellow surges on his mailèd breast.
    Thy foam is on his beard, he gains the land,
    Thou Roman! and I stretch him forth my hand.

XXIX.

Who rests within this soil must slumber well,
    For on it the sad, earnest past hath shed
    Its holiest consecration, and the dead
Know it, and beneath can feel its spell;
To die, then, and to rest in Roman mould
    Were something: wearing into all the past,
    Whose glory like a sunbeam backward cast
Might keep the heart from ever growing cold.
It is as if the spirit of ancient Rome
    Unveiling all its glory, cried—"Come ye
And look upon me, but in looking die,
And let thy dust within my shadow lie,
While the soul flying from its first found home,
    Comes to me with the dreams it had of me."

XXX.

I lean back. I am ripe for dreams to-day;
    For who that rests beneath a sky like this
    Could shirk their soft existence, and so miss
Communings that etherealise the clay?
Rome is her own wide grave, and there can be
    No aftermath for her. The wise and good—
    Her foster-children—claim'd it as they stood.
Through the spent avalanche of the years I see
The light of each great soul, and, dreaming on,
    What Rome was sinks, as if to make a base
To the grand structure of the mind which God
    Seals as a symbol of Himself alone;
I enter; though I cannot see His face
    I know that I am near His pure abode.

XXXI.

Roma! Roma! Roma! Thus my lips
    Took the soft language of the glowing skies
    Of Italy. A stranger with dim eyes
Takes leave of thee, and like a shadow slips
From thy fair presence. With me I had brought
    Dreams of my boyhood, and I take away
    Others of sadder colour, as one may
When leaving the still room wherein our thought
Is with the sainted dead. But as I go
    I feel that ever after in my breast
    What Rome has been, and is, will take its rest,
And be a picture in me, with the glow
    Of sunset over it. Her mighty great
    Are with her to the end, above her fate.

XXXII.

The ruins of years—nay, Time himself—are here:
  I sit within them; but the brooding heart
  Wanders to Florence, to become a part
Of one, by whom, as we walk with our peer,
Sorrow went forth, nor left him till he died—
  Dante, upon whose cheek the grime of hell
  Seems half-wash'd off by the hot tears that fell
At sight of those that wail'd on either side.
He stood in heaven with that spot, but still
  The effluence from the celestial glow
  Of her who led him, made him feel the ill
  He left behind on earth. So stern yet meek
He went, not looking up, but bent his brow,
Conscious of the black stain upon his cheek.

XXXIII.

Florence! they cried, and as they spoke, I stood,
  And said—the quick tears filling up my eyes—
  Dante's lost city, which, with life-long sighs,
He yearn'd for in his exile, whence the brood
Of factions drove him. Had he found this home,
  One marvel less had been in books, and we
  Had seen no vision of the world to be,
Or known how far thought can be made to roam.
Dante's lost city! In these words we feel
  That lone worn spirit of his break forth in sighs,
And all our own half-smitten, till we reel,
  Seeing those eyes that seem so sunk and dull,
By looking on the gnawing of the skull,*
  Or blinded by the light of Paradise.

* La bocca sollevò dal fiero pasto
Quel peccatór, &c.—*Inferno.* Canto, xxxiii.

XXXIV.

Infinite sorrow, like a martyr's crown,
   Rests upon Dante. Looking from those eyes
That hide it not, though ever looking down,
   While those of Beatrice pierce the seventh skies.
Dost thou remember how we stood, and kept
   Our gaze upon the picture where the two
Were thus seen? She so pure and sweet to view:
He earthy, though within the heavens. I wept,
   Touch'd with the spirit of his grief, which spoke
To mine, until when from my trance I woke
I heard thee say—" In these two are express'd
   The higher and the lower nature, which,
   Being within us, we are claimed by each,
Like the two spirits in Faust's weary breast."

XXXV.

The rapt diviner poets struggle still,
   Like angels with one wing, to reach their heaven,
Though it may be with dust-soil'd pinion, till
   Death pities, and the other wing is given.
This earth is not for them, and when they come
   They stand as strangers, till, at last, they speak
Their mission in keen melody, through which
   Floats the deep yearning to regain their home,
Which, though they stand on earth, is in their reach,
   Till the light fades upon their brow and cheek;
Then heaven takes back its own that was so sweet.
   In this thought I can lie in Italy,
   And roll aside part of the sky, and see
Beatrice with Dante at her feet.

XXXVI.

In England now! and yet the Rome I left
   Follows me like a shadow. I can still
   Limn forth those ruins, which men's hands and skill
Made for the ages. But the Goth hath cleft
His ruthless way, and time has follow'd him.
   The Forum, Colosseum, Capitol,
The Cæsar's palaces, now dark and dim,
   The Circus and the Pantheon, the soul
   Of what Rome was, her temples, all is dead
But that which was of heaven; the far thought
   Of poet, sage, historian, still have part
   In all the present; Sculpture bows her head,
   And full-eyed Painting, with her glorious art,
Puts down her footstep, hallowing all the spot.

XXXVII.

To-morrow I will be with thee, and break
   Upon thy silence, and thy treasured looks.
   In fancy I can see thy eager looks
And hear thy sudden questions, as we take
Our evening walk adown the little street.
   How did I feel when in the evening hour
   I stood within the Forum, with the power
Of Cicero upon me? Did my feet
   Half shrink to touch the ground where the abodes
   Of men had been who were fit mates for gods?
And last—What have you brought me? For I crave
   Some souvenir of fallen Rome, and I,
   Knowing thy early worship, will reply—
A wither'd violet from Keats's grave.

RABELAIS.

J'AIME *Monsieur François Rabelais*, that
    Rough, shoulder-shrugging, laughing Frenchman,
Who struts about, broad, red, and fat,
    With humour for his constant henchman;
Who shoots his wit like arrows out,
    Which goes straight home, like shoulder-smiters,
Then shrugs himself and wheels about—
    The Falstaff of his country's writers.

Your Fénélon can smoothly glide,
    Harmoniously in polish'd setting;
And Racine, who for sorrow died
    Because his monarch took to petting;
And Molière—witty dog—who caught
    The lighter nature of his brothers,
And, like Greek Aristophanes, taught
    How much of spleen broad laughter smothers.

Then keen Voltaire, who sniff'd and tried
    All things by the test of suspicion,
Who, holding a free lance, could ride
    At aught without an intermission;
And yet for all his witty ways
    Could not by any form of pleading,
Write a *lust-spiel*, so Richter says
    In *Hesperus*, which is toughish reading.

But, *corps de Dieu*, this Rabelais stands
    With broad and rubicon complexion,

And tickles you as if with hands,
    Until you catch his own infection.
He cares not for your priests or kings,
    That strut upon this stage so fickle,
But holds them both as legal things
    To poke his fingers at and tickle.

Of course, the faults that mark'd his age
    Are found in this bluff, jolly toper,
Who says things very far from sage,
    Which to translate would be improper.
Yet innocent enough they lie
    Behind their old French style of cover,
That costs you many a weary sigh
    Before you can get rightly over.

But still you like him in your mind,
    And hang upon each wordy duel;
And laugh with him, and slip behind
    Grandgousier and Pantagruel.
Frère Jean, too, has a spell to cast
    About you, very deep and daring—
Frère Jean, that rough iconoclast,
    Who fells opponents with his swearing.

Comment, frère Jean, vous jurez? sighs
    A friend, who thought that habit shocking;
C'est pour orner mon langage, cries
    This testy Jean, so fond of joking.
Poor Hood, from Deutchland writing back,
    Said Luther's statue, to his liking,
Was counterpart of Friar Jack—
    A compliment not wise or striking.

A nos moutons, it were for me
    A task to ferret out the meaning
That lies behind *la joyeuse vie*,
    De Pantagruel and its screening.
Yet, *inter nos*, it might be said,
    Apart from all his classic chaffing,
That Rabelais sometimes shakes his head,
    As if our duty were—not laughing.

But yet, as Pierre Dupont holds,
    The mighty *soif* with which he rages
Is but that high thirst which enfolds
    Itself around the lore of sages.
That all his praise of golden wine,
    And reeling Bacchic invitations,
But symbolise Minerva's shrine,
    By which we ought to pour libations.

Then setting François in the light
    Of teacher in his way, and putting
His *grand peut-être* out of sight,
    As not our present purpose suiting;
But thinking that his moral's pith
    Is broad, and very far from mystic,
I laugh myself, and finish with
    A stanza Pantagruelistic.

Come, *buveurs*, jolly topers, drink
    From golden wisdom's flowing sources,
Until like her own owl we blink,
    And reel with all her heavenward forces.
Ha, parlons de boire and sup,
    Le bon Dieu is the boundless giver;
Ventre de Saint Quenet, drink up,
    And let the world grow wise for ever.

THE LAST SWEET WALK.

A TENDER light, when I look back,
   Is all that I can see
Of that sweet time and that sweet walk—
   The last she took with me.

The day was bright, and sweet, and clear,
   As those they have above;
A day whose birth was not for care,
   But for all peace and love.

Along the wood's green edge we stept,
   Our vision downward bent;
And still the leaves above us kept
   A murmur as we went.

At last we reach'd the spot where she,
   In early summer days,
Had watch'd the sun all quietly
   Go down with golden blaze.

Then down we sat upon the seat,
   So placed that we could view
For miles the landscape in the heat,
   The river running through.

And near, the stream, with babbling speech,
   Leapt o'er its pebbled bed;
While hazels with their fruit in reach
   Hung ripe above our head.

We heard at times the low, sweet call
  Of birds distinct and brief;
And now and then the ghostly fall
  Of the red autumn leaf.

We sat, and yet I could not speak,
  But still as the soft air
Look'd wistfully upon her cheek,
  And on the shadow there.

That shadow said, "This is not life
  But a pure flame within,
That will withdraw from earthly strife
  Before it suffer sin."

I mused and thought, How sweet the breath
  That now lies on the earth,
As if the very step of death
  Were a lone thing of dearth.

The fields, the trees, the singing brook,
  The very clouds I see,
Have on a universal look
  Of full felicity.

And yet to me their golden pride
  Brings thoughts that ache full sore;
For one sweet being at my side
  Will look on them no more.

She knew my thought; for, turning round
  With a sweet smile, she said—
"Deem not that death can give one wound,
  Or fill me with one dread.

I look upon the sky above,
   On all things here below,
And take unto myself their love,
   And daily stronger grow.

And now upon the brink of death,
   With a mute sense of rest
I stand, and feel that when my breath
   Has left, I will be blest.

Nor do I feel one bitter thought
   Start up within, that I
Should fix with early death my lot
   And life's rich treasures nigh.

For well I know the same sweet light
   That wraps the earth this hour
Is far above without its night,
   And tripled in its power.

Therefore in hope and love I wait
   The hour, the end, when I
From out the dust will rise in state
   To immortality.

But when I pass into the things
   That are, and in thy breast
Am held but as a voice that sings
   At night, when all is rest:

If one frail word of mine should rise
   And strike thy inner ear,
And I should pass before thine eyes,
   As I to-day appear:

Know that I come to aid the good
   Which is but yet begun;
To teach thee all that fortitude
   Without which nought is won.

And now when other years rejoice,
   Like those that went before,
O may they keep alive a voice
   That sounds on earth no more."

She, whose sweet spirit could not err,
   Sleeps from our sorrow free,
Yet the same sun that smiled on her
   Shines down this day on me.

DINGLE DOOZIE.

DINGLE, dingle doozie,
   Hoo he lauchs to see't
Whirlin' roun' an' up an' doon,
   Frae his heid an' feet.
Keep his dumpy fingers in,
   Dinna touch the lowe;
Dingle, dingle doozie,
   Burn his curly pow.

What a spurlin' wi' his feet
   An' hotchin' on my knee,
Divin' at the burnin' stick,
   Then lookin' up at me;

No anither thing will please,
   Though we turn the hoose,
Dingle, dingle doozie,
   Burn the nose o' puss.

Pussie's wiser than the bairn,
   Gies the stick a cuff,
Ruffles up her back an' tail,
   An' starts to girn an' fuff;
Weel she kens what sparks will dae,
   No like this wee man;
Gudesake, hoo did that come roun'?
   There he's burn'd his han'.

Rin an' fetch his faither's stick
   That nane gets but the wean;
Or mak' the big pat lid a girr,
   An' birl't on the hearth-stane.
Nasty doozie! tak' the fire
   For daurin' tae dae this;
Is his han'ie better noo,
   Since mammy's gien't a kiss?

What are we but bairnies still,
   Every way we turn?
Scram'lin' after lowin' sticks,
   But to get a burn.
Bairnies sittin' saxty years
   On mither life's braid knee,
Watchin' dingle doozies whirl
   Roun' us till we dee.

IS WEE JAMIE WAUKIN' YET?

IS wee Jamie waukin' yet?
    Lyin' unco lang;
Better cuddlin' in his bed
    When his mammy's thrang.
Here he's comin' ow'r the stock,
    Warstlin' a' his lane;
Toddle forrit to the fire,
    Mammy's sturdy wean.

What a fire to mak' him glower,
    An' rub his een sae bauld;
Sic a fire was never seen
    For a bairn that's cauld.
Here are buities, pit them on,
    For fear a coal micht spark;
Bell, ye muckle idle thing,
    Dinna lift his sark.

Fetch his poshie an' his milk,
    Set them on the chair;
What a bowlfu' for a wean!
    An' nane to get a share.
Dinna skail them, like a man,
    But sup them snodly oot;
Then mak' Johnnie your wee horse,
    To pu' your cairt aboot.

Keep us! what a hurry noo,
    Doon he flings the spune;

Is his wee bit kitey fou'?
    Let his mammy fin'.
There, noo, get his cairt; but stop,
    Sic a face as that
Wad mak' oor neebor's doggie bark,
    An' fricht the verra cat.

I hear him half-way up the yaird,
    Cryin' "Wo" an' "Hup;"
But, mercy! what a squeel frae Jock :
    The plague has used the whup.
I fling the dish-cloot frae my han'
    An' hurry oot tae see :
Just as I thocht; thae bairns that strike,
    They fairly puzzle me.

READING THE BOOK.

I SAT by night and read the Book,
    Till doubt was mingled with my look,

And dimness lay before my eyes,
As mists in hollows form and rise.

"So dark, so very dark," I said,
And shut the Book and bow'd my head;

Then lo! I felt a wondrous light
Behind me, making all things bright;

While a clear voice, like some refrain,
Said—" Ope the Book, and read again."

I open'd up its leaves, and lo !
Each page was living with the glow

Of some great Presence undefin'd,
Yet standing in its place behind.

Methought that as I read the Word
Each leaf turn'd of its own accord,

And all the meaning fair and clear,
As pebbles through the stream appear,

Lay to my eyes, that saw beneath
Each sentence lie without its sheath.

I raised my head, and spoke in fear—
"This is God's Book, and very clear."

Then, lo! the light behind me fled,
But left a clear, sweet voice that said—

" Read thou not like to him who sees
Evolving mists of mysteries,

But like to him whose heart perceives
God's finger turning o'er the leaves !"

DAVID GRAY.

"In Eden every flower is blown. Amen."—His own epitaph.

I was lately sent by a friend a copy of the new edition of David Gray's poems, now issued by Maclehose. I had read them years before, and on reading them again, a desire to add a tribute, however feeble, to their worth and freshness grew within me. The result was this poem. What is in the book can be seen by all, but that which slumbers with him of his early dreams and high hopes can never be known. He sleeps his last sleep in Kirkintilloch Churchyard, one of " the inheritors of unfulfilled renown."

A HAPPY time in my young life—when dreams
    Ran in sweet thrills through all my eager frame—
Came back again with all its golden gleams,
    Like summer's sunset with its beams of flame,

And, reaching outward, brought with broad desire
    The old thoughts and fancies that like jewels lay
In their own dust, to brighten like a fire
    When touch'd, and that sweet touch was—DAVID GRAY.

For years before, when he was fresh in death,
    The echo of his short existence came,
And touching mine bore like a meadow breath,
    A giant wish to scale the steeps of fame.

And gathering round this, as a high chief truth,
    Came proud-will'd Titan dreams, and hopes that spring,
Like tropic birds, from out the heart of youth,
    And those ethereal vatic souls who sing.

So came his life to me, with all its sweets,
    And breathing through me with a kindred tone,
Led me, as one is led by Roman Keats,
    Through fits and dreams that once had been my own.

I wept true tears of fellowship, as through
    Fair dreams and sweet, though wither'd, hopes rose up;
Not death, but something beautiful to view—
    A wreath'd Apollo with inverted cup.

For God laid His own hands upon his head
    And drew him nearer, so with nobler look
He stands to us pure-toned in all he said
    And sung in this death-gift of his, this book.

Lo! as I once more turn its leaves, so rife
    With the proud beatings of that eager heart,
Again, like wither'd violets, all his life
    Stirs up and hangs above his passionate art.

And, reading on, we ever stop to ask,
    What if this "piece of childhood thrown away"
Had grown to manhood working at its task,
    Till the flush'd evening sober'd into gray?

Vain question—for the Sphinx-like years are mute,
    And will not answer, but this promise seen,
Will ever stand a statue veil'd to shoot
    White hands to all the fond what might have been.

But he is in the shadows where no cloy
    Can enter. Let us leave him to his rest;
Knowing that years ago the eager boy
    Has ripen'd in the warmth of God's own breast,

And thrilling with full growth of heavenly powers,
    Hears the deep melody of sphere to sphere;
And throbbing with that music not like ours,
    Stands with his back to what he left us here:

For other songs are his. But ours are still
   Those his lips utter'd of his hopes and fears,
Dropt like a stone in the lake with unripe skill,
   To send a tiny ripple through the years.

Then flow, thou Luggie, with a softer gush;
   Thou wert his boyhood's worship; flow along,
While the kind years grant him his deathbed wish,
   And make him the fifth name in unfledged song.

So let him sleep his early sleep; we know
   What slumbers with him all untold to time;
The crush'd flower gives forth odour, but will blow
   No more into the fulness of its prime.

Therefore, O friend, who still had thought of me
   In the city's whirl, if this poor song of mine
Bring thy dead friend—for he was dear to thee—
   Nearer, or lay in thought his hands in thine,

It will be double joy to me that I,
   A poor rough singer in my own rough way,
Should lay this rhythmic offering with a sigh
   On the young Schiller of dreamers—DAVID GRAY.

IN KIRKCONNEL OLD CHURCHYARD.

Each in his narrow cell forever laid,
The rude forefathers of the hamlet sleep.—Gray's Elegy.

THE mist lies on Glen Aymer hill,
  Listless as if asleep,
Below the silence quivers still
  With bleatings of the sheep.

I hear the curlew's sudden call,
  The lapwing follows suit;
The little streamlet's tiny fall,
  The distance makes half mute.

Afar upon the hills I hear
  The shepherd's whistle keen;
A dog's bark faintly strikes the ear
  From uplands fresh and green.

And here, beneath the summer sky,
  With all my thoughts at rest,
The sunshine falling from on high
  On brow and face and breast

I lie, within the old churchyard
  Of fair Kirkconnel town,
Where simple names can yet be read
  On stones half-worn and brown.

I take my knife and scratch the moss
  From names and dates, to see
A vanish'd time restore its loss
  And hold converse with me.

O wondrous dates that find a tongue,
  And ever speak in strange
Sweet syllables, distinctly sung,
  The mystery of change!

Close by my feet, half-hid in grass,
  The skull and cross-bones peer,
For man, where'er he lives, must pass
  To death by symbols drear.

O mighty mystery, unread
  By sage's tongue or pen,
The sloping sunshine overhead,
  Beneath the bones of men!

I rise and pace the narrow round,
  Then come like one in search,
And step across the circling mound
  That marks the vanish'd church.

Within the mound I lie, and see
  Before me in the wall
The narrow gate that used to be,
  Ere time had wasted all.

Now, if within my dreaming brain
  The German Uhland's pow'r
Could be, then would I paint again
  That Sabbath and that hour;

Or, if this tree whose shadows bland
    Are on my face, could be
A voice to whisper things, and stand
    A talking tree to me.

But, hush! my eyes are softly shut
    By gently-falling beams,
And underneath their lids are put
    The germ of noonday dreams.

O wondrous mystery, unread
    By tongue of sage or pen,
The happy sunshine overhead,
    Beneath the dust of men!

I sleep, but all my pow'rs are fix'd
    Upon a space half-clear,
Where, partly with dim shadows mix'd,
    Faces rise up and peer.

Then floats the psalm upon the air,
    And all the place around
Is breathing worship everywhere,
    And drinking in the sound.

I, too, join in the soothing song,
    And in the solemn prayer;
I bow together with the throng
    That meet to worship there.

The homely face of sire and wife
    Glows as upon their ear
The promise, quieting all strife,
    Falls soft and sweet to hear.

O faces full of trust and love,
  O looks that had no doubt,
My heart beat like a saint's above,
  And grew at once devout!

Beside me aged mothers bent,
  Whose lives had reach'd their term;
And one sweet bride in fondness leant
  Upon her husband's arm.

I saw the blushes on her cheek,
  The light within her eye,
The thoughts that were too fond to speak,
  But utter'd in a sigh.

Sweet maidens in their bloom were there,
  Within whose drooping eyes
The sun of dawning love was fair,
  As stars within the skies.

And youths, strong limb'd, with frank, bold look,
  That seem'd to pierce beyond
The future darkness, and rebuke
  Aught wishing to despond.

And still the white-hair'd pastor's voice
  Fell on the ear, and still
A curlew would make sudden noise,
  And swoop around the hill.

But now they rise with bended head,
  The old and young to hear
The simple benediction said
  In reverential fear.

Then through the gateway open'd wide
They take their winding way—
Sire, mother, bridegroom, and sweet bride,
Youth, maid, and children gay.

Last came the pastor, and I saw
His white hair in the wind
Move, as he turn'd in holy awe
And left the church behind.

Then all the silence came again,
And, for the want of sound,
I woke : my heart was full of pain,
And sadly I look'd round.

I heard the swaying of the tree,
I saw the grasses wave,
By fits on either side of me,
Above each lonely grave.

The sheep were on the mountain side,
Dotting its breast like snow ;
I heard the low of kine, descried
In meadows far below.

"O dead !" I said, "sleep on and rest
In all thy quiet here ;
The great world, in its eager quest,
Can never come anear."

But, lo ! from out the distant vale
An engine's whistle keen
Comes sharply up, as to assail
The silence that had been.

O mighty mystery, unread
By tongue of sage or pen,
The change that rolls with iron tread
Above the dust of men!

MARY.

ROSES fade, and why not you?
   Mary, in whose eyes we view
Sweetest fancies peeping through,

So that unto us they seem
Colours in a fairy's dream—
Shaded pool of woodland stream,

Where the rounded pebbles lie,
Underneath its melody:
Thus within thine earnest eye

All the happy thoughts we see
Rise in their sweet purity,
Speaking evermore of thee.

Roses fade, but thy decay
Must be very far away;
Angels live more than a day:

Yet if thou shouldst link thy fate
To the rose's blushing state,
Thou canst never shame thy mate.

Like the rose, if Death should come
And bear thee to his silent home,
Where thy kindred spirits roam,

Thou shalt leave, as a relief
Behind thee, calming down our grief,
All the fragrance of its leaf:

Thus within our hearts shall be,
For ever as a type of thee,
The incense of thy memory.

OVER THE SEA, ANNIE.

THE wings of the dear old past, Annie,
    Are falling over me,
And again my thoughts take their flight, Annie,
    Over the sea to thee.
Over the sea, over the sea,
    To that quaint, gray, quiet town,
Where you walk in the evening light, Annie,
    As the golden sun sinks down.

And later, when twilight begins, Annie,
    And the shadows grow deep and long,
Like whispers of spirits in dreams, Annie,
    I hear you singing my song—
Singing my song, and the old, sweet words,
    Like incense of angels rise;
And their music is in my heart, Annie,
    While the tears are in my eyes.

O ! just to see you again, Annie,
    To walk with your hand in mine ;
To stand by your side and look, Annie,
    Into those eyes of thine—
Into the thoughts and the depths of those eyes,
    As I did two years ago,
When we stood by the old, gray tower, Annie,
    With the woods and the fields below.

But the wish sinks away as it forms, Annie ;
    Only from over the sea,
When the twilight is coming down, Annie,
    You are singing that song to me—
Singing that song, and the dear, old words,
    Like the incense of angels rise,
And their music is in my heart, Annie,
    While the tears are in my eyes.

THE BOWGIE MAN.

DID ye see the Bowgie man
    Stan'in' at the door ?
Ae big pock flung owre his back,
    Anither doon afore.
Did ye hear him cryin' oot,
    As he geid a knock—
" Mithers fash'd wi' steerin' weans,
    Pit them in my pock ?"

Gudeness, what has brocht him here,
    Giein' fowk a fricht,
Speerin' after weans, an' look—
    Eicht o'clock at nicht.
Hae I ony in the house?
    Here's ane on my knee,
Winna let his claes come aff,
    Or steek an e'e for me.

Bowgie, stan'in' at the door,
    Where is't that ye keep
Souple rogues that row aboot,
    An' never think on sleep?
Hear him turn the han'le roun',
    Then anither knock,
" In anaith the big mill wheel,
    Tied up in my pock."

Bowgie, if a bairn we ken
    Says he'll cuddle doon,
Wull ye leave oor door, an' gang
    Farrer up the toon?
Hear him cryin' oot again,
    As he snowks aboot—
" If he's happit owre the heid
    I daurna pu' him oot."

Bowgie, tak' some ither door,
    Here ye'll come nae speed;
Mammy's bairn has cuddled doon,
    Happit owre the heid.
If ye come anither nicht,
    What a fricht ye'll get!
Gar his faither cut your pocks,
    An' chase ye through the yett.

Mony a bowgie man atweel
  We hae cause to fear,
Comes an' knocks, and axes things
  We dinna want to hear.
Like the bairns, when ilka knock
  Brings some ill-dune deed,
We gang about an' never min',
  If happit owre the heid.

THE WEARY WEIRD.

The following ballad is founded upon the superstitious ideas which formerly existed in the minds of the simple but ignorant peasantry with regard to old churches. They held that if any one laid hands upon wood or stone of an old church, the wrath of God was sure to fall upon him. This was generally manifested by the hand and arm withering, or by sudden death.

THE Nith has a weird, weird soun' the nicht,
  As it swurls through the big black pool,
An' the win' comin' doon through the Piper's Cleuch
  Has a waefu' soun' o' dool.

An' thrice hae I heard, as I stood by the door,
  A soun' like a funeral bell,
An' my bluid ran prinklin' frae heid to fit
  As I heard its eerie knell.

I thocht the Nith took a deeper sough
  At that waefu', wailin' soun',
While the reid, reid streamers within the north
  They glimmer'd up an' doon.

They glimmer'd up till, abune my heid,
    They faded an' sunk away,
But aye the soun' o' that eerie knell
    Cam' doon frae the auld kirk brae.

The auld kirk wa's an' the moss-grown thrughs
    Are up in the kirkyaird there,
But nae bell has rung on the Sabbath day
    For fifty years an' mair.

Noo, wha can be pu'in' that unseen rape
    In the mirk, mirk hoor o' the nicht?
An' wha can be ringin' that unseen bell
    That has gien me sic a fricht?

Alake the day! has the time come roun'
    For that unseen bell to swing?
O! weel I min' hoo my bluid ran cauld
    When first I heard it ring.

I ken wha it is that pu's the rape
    That never yet has been seen,
An' I ken wha is ringin' the bell, though nane
    Hings the auld bare wa's atween.

But sit ye doon in the big airm-chair,
    An' lean your back to the wa',
An' I'll tell ye the tale o' the auld kirk bell,
    An' the death o' Simon Gaw.

When the roof o' the kirk up there fell in,
    An' nae mair, on the Sabbath day,
The douce, plain herds and the kintra folk
    Cam' together to sing an' pray.

Then a sayin' gaed through the kintra-side,
   That whaever took stick or stane
Frae the kirk wad never dae weel through life,
   An' his airm wad shrink to the bane.

But a deeper curse wad come doon on the heid
   O' him wha took the bell—
It wad swing an' ring in his ears until
   It brocht his funeral knell.

For the kirk, they said, is God's ain house,
   Though built wi' stane an' lime,
An' never a han' may touch roof or wa'
   Save the unseen han' o' Time.

But little they care for the holy things
   Wha serve in their heart the deil,
An' worship nocht but the gowd they mak',
   An' their ain narrow, warldly weal.

Sae, in spite o' the curse that was spoken oot,
   Ere a twalmonth had time to speed,
They began to pu' down the auld kirk wa's
   To serve their selfish greed.

First the Laird o' Glenheid took away some stanes,
   To pit his byre-en' richt;
But a week scarce had gane when nae coo had he
   To rowte in the byre at nicht.

Then the farmer o' Meikle Knowe took a door
   On his ain big barn to swing,
But ever after, until he dee'd,
   He gaed wi' his airm in a sling.

An' never man or woman saw
    That airm o' his laid bare ;
But weel they ken'd that the bane was black,
    An' nae flesh or muscle there.

Young Tamson, the Laird o' Whinny Glen,
    Was the next to tak' away
Some wud for an oot hoose to beild his stirks,
    But he saw nae anither day.

For the Nith rase up as he cross'd the ford,
    An' man an' horse gaed doon,
An' were faun' next day by the Nailer's Craig
    Where the swurl gangs roun' an' roun'.

Sae the curse that was spoken aboot the kirk
    By auld grey-heided men
Fell on a' wha had ta'en away stick or stane,
    An' they cam to a waefu' en'.

But what was the horror o' young an' auld,
    When the neebours began to tell
That the nicht afore ane had speel'd the wa',
    An' had stolen away the bell !

O meikle, meikle wrath, I wat,
    Was in the hearts o' a' ;
" An' wha can hae dune the deed ?" they ask'd,
    While they thocht on Simon Gaw.

But they never cam' oot wi' his name, I trow,
    Though it lay in their heart an' heid ;
" It will sune be seen, for the curse," they said,
    " Canna pass by siccan a deed."

An' aye after this, at a certain time,
    Auld Simon Gaw was seen
To gang aboot, as if pu'in' a rape,
    While a mad look cam' frae his een.

His airms gaed up an' his airms gaed doon,
    While his mouth took many a shape;
"The curse has fa'en on him at last," they cried,
    "An' his weird's to pu' the rape."

O weary, weary's the weird atweel,
    That ilka ane has to dree,
Wha lays his han's on God's holy things,
    An' thinks that He canna see.

Sae the curse fell on Simon lang an' sair,
    For stealin' the auld kirk bell;
But he never loot on to man o' his sin,
    Though ae nicht he had to tell.

The Nith had an eerie sough that nicht,
    Like that we hear the noo;
An' the streamers away in the strange blue north
    Grew bricht an' white to view.

They glimmer'd upward in flauchts o' licht,
    Then spread their han's o'erheid;
While ae clud wan'er'd away frae the rest,
    Stood still in a sea o' reid.

A licht was seen in the auld kirkyaird—
    It aye gaed roun' an' roun',
Then gleam'd like a star frae abune the place
    Where the bell had been ta'en doon.

THE WEARY WEIRD.

An' aye a soun' gaed through the air,
    But it wasna the soun' o' a bell,
Nor the sough o' the Nith, but what it could be
    Nae mortal man could tell.

It cam' frae the auld kirk up on the knowe,
    An' it seem'd to dee away
Ow'r the tap o' the hoose where Simon Gaw
    On his waefu' deathbed lay.

Few, few were the neebours aboot the door
    That cam' to speir for his weal,
For little trock could they hae wi' ane
    Wha had sellt himsel' to the deil.

But at nicht, when the dark, dark hours set in,
    Anither neebour an' me
Gaed doon to sit up through the eerie nicht—
    The last that Simon wad see.

We sat, an' we watch'd the shadows lie
    On his thin an' ghastly face,
Till within an hoor o' the stroke o' twal,
    An' then a change took place.

A strange, wild look came into his een,
    An' a reid, unholy licht;
While afore we could lay oor han's on him,
    He sat on his bed upricht.

An' his airms gaed up an' his airms gaed doon,
    As if pu'in' at some string,
While a' at aince, at the heid o' the bed,
    A bell began to ring.

Then he lookit roun' as he heard the soun',
    An' cried wi' a' his micht—
" I stole, an' I sellt that bell for gowd,
    That will ring me away this nicht."

Then his airms gaed up an' his airms gaed doon,
    As if ringin' that unseen bell,
An' reider the licht grew within his een
    As he heard that awfu' knell.

I turn'd my back to that dreid, dreid sicht,
    But my heart was sae fu' o' fear
That I fell by the bed at my neebour's feet,
    An' hadna power to steer.

An' aye the bell keepit ringin' on,
    Till at the stroke o' twal'
It ceased; an' I rase, as beneath a weicht,
    Wi' my body dooble faul'.

But whaten a sicht had I to see—
    May I never see like o't mair!
Auld Simon Gaw lay deid on his bed,
    Wi' baith his airms in the air.

An' the same reid licht was within his een—
    It lickit his lips aroun';
It burn'd oor han's as we gruppit his airms
    An' tried to lay them doon.

But afore his corpse was in last white claes,
    We twa were forced to bide,
An' keep doon the airms till the shroud was on,
    For they aye rase up frae his side.

O mony an awfu' doom, atweel,
   Comes doon on the heids o' men,
But the weird that Simon Gaw had to dree
   Was the warst in a' fowk's ken.

An' aye when the nicht o' his death comes roun',
   Strange soun's gang through the air,
An' a bell tolls on frae the auld kirk wa's,
   For Simon Gaw is there.

He pu's an' pu's at an unseen rape—
   At an unseen bell that rings;
For a weary weird fa's on ilka ane
   Wha steals God's holy things.

Sae let us keep min' o' auld Simon Gaw,
   An' act that there may be
Nae bell ringin' on at oor ain bed heid
   When we lay us doon to dee.

CITY AND VILLAGE.

ONCE again within the city, 'mid its multitudinous din,
   Stand I, while, as sinks a leaf when left by the uncertain wind,
So the daily village quiet, and the calm I had within,
   Shrinks before the magic contact of the ever-shaping mind.

In the village life is sluggish, waking up but for a space,
   As the engines shriek and whistle down by hill and wooded glen;
But here a mightier striving stamps itself upon my race—
   Here are all the active ages, and the tramp of busy men.

Then away with daily labour, thoughts of books or weary rhyme,
  Let me plunge into this whirlpool rolling on in mad unrest—
Let me, Faust-like, have the weal of men in all the coming time,
  That its triumph may strike vigour through the soul within my breast.

Hush ! we spoke not of the sorrow that upon their joys will peer,
  As the huge unshapen monster glared in on pale Frankenstein,
Edging life's uncertain smile with all the drapery of a tear,
  And placing in the cup the drop that dulls and drugs the wine.

But heed not this, and think that, in the rolling on of years,
  The slow whirlpool of sure change will lift this life still higher up,
Till it leave behind its apehood, and its daily load of fears,
  And drink existence gladly as if angels held the cup.

Far apocalyptic touches that unveil the years to be,
  Show this in ecstatic glimpses, as when mists upon a hill
Lift their trailing arms of whiteness till, as in a dream, we see
  A summer gush of glory lying hid behind them still.

Is the pencil of broad Hogarth still to keep its biting truth,
  And for ever flash its satire on the world's sweat-blinded sight?
Are we still to stumble onward on a pathway all unsmooth,
  Like a Cyclops in his cavern smitten with the loss of light?

Ay, the time will come, my brothers, though it lies behind far hope,
  Yet faint flashes rise up from it, like the northern lights we see;
Then, while all the ages come to widen out the mighty scope,
  Let us lap ourselves in dreams of what our fellow-men will be.

Look not back with idle murmur lying fretting on thy lips,
  That which lies behind is but the crude world's shadow in dull light;
Look thou forward where the sunshine from a kindlier heaven slips,
  Cheering on thy kind to wider vantage-grounds for truth and right.

The far ages bristling upward, waiting for their unborn men,
　Have in them the golden blossom of the seed we sow in fear;
Wider growths of thought and ripeness, nobler tasks for brain and
　　pen,
　Fuller brotherhood in all that perfects us to manhood here.

Heart! to see our future fellows standing on our present gain,
　Which we wrench'd from the stern centuries, and Samson-like
　　made ours,
Shaping, with a larger forethought and a finer grasp of brain,
　Pathways to the purer use of life and all our human powers.

Theirs shall be our slow improvement rising up to perfect bloom,
　Through the centuries niggard of it, like the aloe with its bud;
It shall bring new modes of thinking that shall all the old entomb,
　Building up a higher channel for the rushing on of good.

For our fellows striving onward, though they wear the stain of toil,
　Ever yearn to shape out goals to which their better natures tend;
And their good within shoots upward, like a plant within the soil,
　To the higher, grander freedom, to the nobler godlike end.

Then let change come striking outward, with soft touch or sudden
　　shock,
　Let the years glide by, if we can feel that in the lapse of time,
As a leaping mountain torrent through decades can smooth the rock,
　We are growing better, wiser, surer of the foot to climb.

For the struggle in the climbing will be hard and ill to bear;
　Each one, like the souls in Dante, wearing cloaks and hoods of lead;
But for ever as we struggle, with half breath to breathe a prayer,
　From above we hear the echo of another brother's tread.

For the selfless souls amongst us, hearted with the heart of Christ,
　Ever turn and beckon onward that their strength may be our own;

And we hear their potent watchwords, which, if we could still resist,
   It were shame upon our foreheads burning to the very bone.

All their lives and thoughts are with us, and the strong world's future weal
   Will be shaped by what they fought for, though it may be ere it form
(For it will not take their semblance as soft wax takes on the seal),
   Cycles may rise up, and set in cloudless calm or sudden storm.

But it will be : higher comfort as we labour scarce can be ;
   Mists may rise and wrap it from us, but the mighty darting sun
Will strike heat throughout the shadows till, like phantom shapes they flee,
   Leaving all the good we strove for, and the better laurels won.

Thanks, then, toiling, restless city, that my heart should leap and fill
   With such thoughts to help me onward in my own rough life and toil,
That I see through all this hurry one ennobling purpose still ;
   Dim as yet, but growing brighter, like the mists that leave the soil.

And that purpose still turns brighter at the touch on either hand
   Of my fellow-kind who, with me, hold the same high hope of this,
Each one sets it to that music reaching him where he may stand ;
   But it still keeps ring and measure to the far-off coming bliss.

Teach, then, poet, prophet, priest, with hands stretch'd out to that desire ;
   Ring it forth to toiling men, and waft it over land and sea,
As the rugged Hebrew prophet, while his eyeballs swam in fire,
   Sent down through his vatic brotherhood the Christ that was to be.

Far behind me lies the city, with its ebb and flow of men,
    But the thoughts that came within it are for ever in my breast ;
And they leap up as the engines thunder down by hill and glen,
    Or in my walks at night-time when the village is at rest.

COCKIE-ROOSIE-RIDE.

PIT the bairn on mammy's back,
    Ow'r her shuiders pit his feet ;
Let me grup his wee fat legs,
    While his brithers laugh to see't.
Pit the stules anaith the chairs,
    Clear the hoose on ilka side ;
Maunna fa' when mammy gies
    Her bairn a cockie-roosie-ride.

Is he ready ? Here we gang,
    Jumpin' roun' the hoose wi' glee ;
Stoppin' whiles afore the glass
    To let the lauchin' laddie see.
Losh me, hoo he gecks an' goos,
    An' shogs an' sweys frae side to side ;
Is his heid, like some we ken,
    Turn'd wi' his cockie-roosie-ride.

No ae minute can I stan',
    Roun' the hoose we gang again,
While the rascal tries to mak'
    My mutch-strings ser' him for a rein.

Hoo he kicks an' tries to spur,
    An' thraws his face wi' very pride;
Gudesake ! has he min' o' men
    When at his cockie-roosie-ride.

What's the matter wi' him noo,
    That he's takin' sic a grup,
Signin' wi' the ither han'
    For Jock to han' him up his whup ?
Wad the sorra really strike—
    Bairns are unco ill to guide—
Strike his mammy, on whase back
    He tak's his cockie-roosie-ride ?

There, noo, juist as I had thocht,
    Struck the wa' press wi' his croon ;
Whup an' strings are a' let gae,
    As I boo to set him doon.
What a greetin' bairn, an' yet
    Siccan knocks are ill to bide ;
Bless him, he'll get waur, I doot,
    In life's cockie-roosie-ride.

Dinna greet, but cuddle doon
    Safe an' snug on mammy's knee ;
Cuddle, an' she'll clap his heid,
    An' mak' it better in a wee.
See, he's sabbit into sleep,
    Thinkin' nae what may betide
When he turns a man, an' tak's
    Anither cockie-roosie-ride.

A' this warl's naething mair
    But a ride to rich an' poor ;

Up an' doon we ride oor day
Gettin' mony a fa' an' cloor;
Then at last, when tir'd an' sair
Wi' wan'erin' unco far an' wide,
Quately are we slippit doon
Frae oor cockie-roosie-ride.

GRANNY GREY POW.

AULD Granny Grey Pow,
    Fetch the bairnies in;
Bring them frae the Scaur Heid,
    Where they mak' sic din.
Chase them frae the washin' pool,
    Thrang at skippin' stanes—
Auld Granny Grey Pow,
    Gather hame the weans.

Bring in Rab to get him wash'd,
    Weel I ken the loon
Canna dae unless he be
    Dirt frae fit to croon.
Tam and Wull are just the same,
    For a' I tak' sic pains—
Auld Granny Grey Pow,
    Gather hame the weans.

Fetch my ain wee Jeanie in,
    Mammy's pet o' a';
Jamie, wha aye slips aboot,
    And speaks nae much ava.

Bring them to their cosie bed,
    There to rest their banes—
Auld Granny Grey Pow,
    Gather hame the weans.

Here they come; ill Rab is first
    Tam an' Wull ahin';
Jamie has wee Jeanie's han',
    An' baith begin to rin.
Whaten faces hae they a'—
    Dirt laid on in grains!
Auld Granny Grey Pow,
    Gather hame the weans.

In they toddle, ane by ane;
    Wull, wha's aye the fule,
Quarrels wi' ill Rab aboot
    Whase nicht it's for the stule.
Jeanie hunkers at my feet,
    While sleep upon her gains—
Auld Granny Grey Pow,
    I hae a' my weans.

Auld Granny Grey Pow,
    Steek the door fu' ticht,
No a wean, if I can help,
    Gangs ower the door this nicht.
There they lie in cosie beds,
    The morn's wark in their brains—
Auld Granny Grey Pow,
    Bless my sleepin' weans.

Mony a fit we hae to gang,
    Mony a care to deave;

Joy an' woe are thread aboot
In the wab we weave.
Let us work it to the en',
So that He who reigns
May whisper, when life's gloamin' comes,
" Gather hame the weans."

THE FIDDLER O' BOGLEBRIGGS.

A FIDDLER sits, wha has never been seen,
On the ledgin' o' Boglebriggs ;
An' aye when the clock strikes the midnicht hoor
He plays strathspeys an' jigs.

He plays strathspeys, an' reels, an' jigs,
Like ane at a country fair ;
But never a lad or a lass daur gang
To dance to the music there.

The fowk wha live at the hoose doon bye,
Where the lang road tak's a turn,
Can hear, when they wauken up at nicht,
The sough o' the Bogle Burn.

But alang wi' its sough comes an eerie soun'
They dinna like to hear—
The scrape o' the fiddle, that comes by fits,
Frae the brig sae auld an' drear.

Then the hoolits that bide in the Brocklan' wud
    Flaff roun' wi' an' eerie cry;
While the water kelpies in ilka pool
    Coor doon till it gangs by.

But still on the ledgin' o' Boglebriggs
    That fiddler sits an' plays;
An' never gangs ow'r till the licht begins
    To shine on the Scroglan' Braes.

But listen awee to Eppy Graham,
    Wha bides at the heid o' the glen,
An' she'll tell ye the story aboot that brig
    That has frichten'd weans an' men.

"Lang syne, when a lassie aboot sixteen,
    (I'm ninety this very nicht),
I ran to weddin's, an' kirns, an' balls—
    For my heart was unco licht.

An' aften, an' aften hae I gaen doon
    A country dance wi' glee,
For a stout, stout fiddler led us oot—
    Lang shankit Gibby Fea.

He fiddled at rockins and kintra kirns,
    Where we a' made meikle din;
An' aye at the ball on a Hogmanay,
    When we danced the New Year in.

An' at ane o' the balls my dress was white,
    While the lang, lang ribbons were reid,
And I had a rose that was white as snaw,
    Noddin' bonnie 'bune my heid.

I bore the brag o' that ball, an' John
    Was unco prood aboot me ;
But he's deid these thirty weary years,
    An' noo I scarce can see.

I scarce can gang to the ooter door,
    Yet it seems but a short, short day
Since I gaed to that ball by the side o' John,
    Wha is deid lang syne an' away.

But my time will come, for the hoose is dune,
    An' never ane after me
Will bide in this eerie, eerie place,
    That maun see auld Eppie dee.

But my story is slippin' away frae me,
    At thae daft, daft tricks o' mine,
Yet auld, dune bodies aye wan'er an' dream,
    When they think o' auld lang syne.

Weel, Gibby, ye ken, was unco glib,
    For the luve o' the siller hung
On his lang, narrow face and twinklin' e'e,
    An' on his leein' tongue.

Nae gude ever cam' frae his thin white lips,
    But aye when a pair were cried,
He mummel'd an' lauch'd, though he sat in the kirk,
    An' hotch'd frae side to side.

He lived in a hoose by the Boglebriggs—
    The hoose is nae langer there,
For it tum'led doon on a Sabbath nicht,
    An' was biggit up nae mair.

His wife had a greed that was waur than his—
  She harl'd a' things in,
As if she wad live for hunners o' years,
  An' the warl' never gang dune.

Sae they baith did their best for the sake o' the gear,
  Workin' on baith nicht an' day,
Till the neebors aboot said what gear they had
  Wasna got in an honest way.

But Gibby was foremost at kirns an' balls,
  Wi' his twinklin', parrot e'e;
An' Grizzy his wife gather'd into the hoose,
  For unco greedy was she.

O weel I min' what they baith were like,
  Though I canna bring to min'
What I did yestreen; for unco fresh
  Are the things o' auld langsyne.

I min' the auld black hoose that sat
  No a yaird frae the public road;
I min' when the wa's swey'd an' tum'led in,
  Wi' the roof o' heather an' sod.

An' I min' this story I'm gaun to tell—
  It gaed through the kintra side,
An' was tauld by the herds as they sat on the hills,
  An' was sent baith far an' wide:

Ae Saturday nicht, a wee ere twal',
  As Grizzy an' Gibby sat,
A' at ance cam' a queer, queer knock to the door,
  That wauken'd up the cat.

Her back gaed up, an' her tail grew big,
　　While her een turn'd roun' an' reid ;
" What can ail her the nicht ?" ask'd Gibby, an' shook,
　　Wi' meikle doot, his heid.

Then they heard the door play clank to the wa',
　　An' a fit comin' stampin' ben ;
Then they saw a stranger come bauldly in,
　　But whase face they didna ken.

The cat, wi' ae loup, took up to the laft,
　　An' frae there, where she could see
She sat, but aye on that stranger man
　　She keepit a reid, reid e'e.

Auld Gibby an' Grizzy glower'd fu' lang
　　At the man on their ain hearthstane ;
Then Gibby said, " Od, but ye enter in
　　As if this hoose were your ain."

" I hae come to ask ae favour," he said,
　　" An' sma' will that favour be—
Will ye tak' yer fiddle an' come to the brig,
　　An' play ae reel to me ?"

Then Gibby, shakin' his heid, said, " Na,
　　I canna dae that this nicht,
For it wants na much o' the Sabbath morn,
　　And ye ken it wadna be richt."

The stranger's lips had a queer, queer smile,
　　As he turn'd an' said, " Weel, weel,
A gowden guinea is his this nicht
　　Wha plays me a single reel."

THE FIDDLER O' BOGLEBRIGGS.

Auld Grizzy cockit her lugs at this,
   An' she said, " Gudeman, gudeman,
Can ye no play ae reel to the stranger man,
   An' the fiddle close at your han'?"

Then he thocht awee on the lang, lang nichts
   He had fiddled for half that sum,
Sae he rax'd doon the fiddle that hung on the wa',
   An' he said to the stranger, "Come."

"But first," said the stranger, an' here he laid
   In Gibby's loof a bricht
Roun' guinea, that seem'd as if fresh frae the mint,
   For it gleam'd in the cannle licht.

Sae Gibby sat doon upon Boglebriggs,
   An' put his fiddle in tune,
While the stranger stood stampin' an' shakin' his feet,
   As if wearyin' to begin.

Then the fiddler ask'd, as he lifted the bow,
   "Are ye gaun to dance yoursel'?"
The stranger said something atween his teeth
   That Gibby couldna tell.

But juist as he laid the bow on the strings,
   The brig was shinin' wi' licht,
An' ithers forbye him wha wantit the reel
   Cam' a' at ance into sicht.

An' they danced aboot him an' lap like mad,
   Wi' mony a jump an' squeal,
Cryin', " Speed to the elbow o' him whase greed
   Mak's him fiddle to the deil."

Then Gibby saw horns on the stranger's heid,
    An', lookin' doon to his feet,
He saw he divided the hoof like a stot,
    An' he shook wi' terror to see't.

But aye he fiddled an' couldna stop,
    An' aye they changed the reel,
Cryin', " Speed to the elbow o' him whase greed
    Mak's him fiddle to the deil."

Then they took him doon frae the tap o' the brig—
    His fingers aye keepit the string—
An' they claspit their han's, an' roun' they gaed,
    Like weans at a jingo-ring.

Roun', roun, they gaed wi' an eldritch yell,
    An' still they increased their speed,
Till at last they sank down in a flaff o' lowe,
    Leavin' Gibby lyin' as deid.

Auld Grizzy cam' oot when she heard that yell;
    But what was her fricht to see
Her man streekit oot as they streek the deid,
    An' a dull, dead look in his e'e!

Yet she lifted him up, though she had nae help,
    But, afore she could get him in,
Her breath cam' thick, an' her knees bent doon,
    An' the swat brak' through her skin.

She put him into the bed, an' he lay
    Like ane that had lost his breath—
Never liftin' up han', or openin' e'e,
    Till within an hour o' his death.

An' aye he keepit his richt neive shut,
　　As if haudin' some siller there;
But, gude keep us a'! instead o' the gowd,
　　That clinks an' looks sae fair,

A black, black spot where the guinea had lain
　　Was there, an' a frichtfu' heid,
That the deil had set as a mark on his coin,
　　An' a curse on the fiddler's greed.

But aye he lay streekit, nor lifted an e'e,
　　While Grizzy sat by the bed,
Watchin' a' her lane through the weary nicht,
　　Hearin' things that maunna be said.

For the fiddle that hung in a pouk on the wa'
　　Began to birl an' play,
An' rin ow'r the tune that was play'd on the brig
　　As the fiddler wore away.

What a sicht had Grizzy to see as she look'd,
　　Wi' a fear that death aye brings,
To the fiddle hung up that was playin' on,
　　Though nae bow was across the strings.

Then a' at ance the strings play'd crack,
　　An' she never heard it mair,
For, turnin' roun', she saw Gibby was deid,
　　An' she fell frae aff the chair.

The fowk gaun' by on the Sabbath day
　　To the kirk got an awfu' fricht;
For Gibby and Grizzy baith lay deid—
　　A weird an' fearfu' sicht!

M

But nae fiddle was hingin' up on the wa',
    An' fowk like mysel' still say
That it aye plays at nicht on Boglebriggs
    Till the sun hits the Scroglan' Brae.

An' whaever gangs by at the stroke o' twal',
    Whatever his yerran' may be,
He canna but stop when he hears the soun',
    An' dance as if mad wi' glee.

Sae nae lad or lass, or grown-up man,
    Though ye offer them a' ye hae,
Will gang by the brig at the midnicht hoor,
    When that fiddle begins to play;

For they aye hae min' o' the fiddler's death,
    An' his loof wi' its spot sae black,
An' they winna gang near to Boglebriggs,
    But turn in terror back."

Oh! listen, listen! to Eppy Graham,
    Wha bides at the heid o' the glen:
There is truth in this auld, auld story o' hers,
    For the gude an' the guidin' o' men.

An' the truth is this, that wherever ye gang,
    Let them hide it never sae weel,
A black spot lies on their loof whase greed
    Mak's them fiddle to the deil.

OOR FIRST WEE GRAVES.

THEY were a' roun' aboot us, their hearts licht wi' glee,
  An' the pride an' the talk o' their faither an' me;
We had nae broken link when we lookit aroun',
To sen' through oor hearts sorrow's canker an' stoun'.
The shadow afore hadna come on the hearth
To dull wi' its gloom their bit prattle an' mirth,
An' ilka bit joy in the heart o' ilk wean
Sent the same happy pride an' sweet thrill through oor ain.

But it wasna to last; for this strange life o' oors
Is made up o' blinks o' dull sunshine an' shooers;
Sae the shadow at last cam' an' fell on the een
O' Jenny, my ain sweet wee dawtie an' queen.
Saft, saft did it fa', like a clud on the hill,
An' wee paidlin' feet an' a sweet voice grew still,
While a gap on the hearth as I turn'd roun' my e'e,
Dumbly spoke o' the sweet link noo broken to me.

There was weicht at my heart I could ne'er get abune,
When I saw a' the rest when the forenicht set in
Gather roun' wi' their stules, to think ae weel ken'd face
Couldna come to my side an' tak' up its auld place;
An', oh! when I heard them speak lown their bit say,
I thocht on a voice that was noo far away;
But I keepit the tears back for sake o' the lave,
An' the kirkyaird doon-by had oor first wee reid grave.

But waes me, the shadow cam' back wi' its wing,
An' wee Jeanie sank doon like a leaf struck in spring,

OOR FIRST WEE GRAVES.

Sair, sair was my wark nicht an' day wi' the wean,
Yet what will a mither no dae for her ain?
But oor wark was in vain, for the saft breathin' nicht
Saw the angel that faulded our bairn frae oor sicht:
Sae anither wee grave in the kirkyaird was made,
An' in't oor sweet bud by the ither was laid.

'Twas oor first close acquaintance wi' ocht o' the kin';
An' deeply it sunk baith on heart an' on min':
It micht be that something no far frae despair
Fell doon on oor hearts an' lay unco cauld there.
For when grief comes it aye brings the shadows that hide
A' the gude we micht see if we flung them aside;
But a wee grave, ye ken, when it haps what we lo'e,
Tak's mithers an unco lang time to see through.

Sae I grew unco wae, at odd times, wi' the thocht,
That keepit me back frae the gude that I socht;
But the rest o' my bairns were aboot me to cheer,
An' I lichten'd mysel' as things lookit mair clear;
While a voice, heard to nane but mysel', in my breist,
Said in saft, soothin' whispers, when sorrow had ceased,
" Ye ne'er wad hae ken'd what sair hearts can contain
If the finger of God hadna lain on your ain."

But ae nicht a dream cam', an' sweet, sweet to me
Was its truth that I grew maist as licht as could be.
I thocht a white angel frae heaven cam' doon,
An' stood on the hearth wi' lang wings faulded roun',
An', oh! but the smile on his lips was fu' sweet,
As he boo'd, an' laid twa gowden links at his feet.
Then I thocht tae mysel', for the meanin' was plain,
God has sent him doon here wi' a link for ilk wean.

Then he flew to the kirkyaird, still leavin' ahin'
The en' o' the links he had brocht frae abune.
An' he stood on the graves o' the twa bairns o' mine,
Lookin' up to his hame he had left but short syne.
But juist for a moment, then saftly an' licht
He rase on braid wings an' soar'd oot o' my sicht;
But aye, frae the hearth to the kirkyaird doon-by,
The links streekit oot an' gaed up to the sky.

There was bliss in my heart when I wauken'd, an' faun'
That the nicht roun' aboot had been stirr'd by God's han',
An' I ken'd He had sent, frae His shadowless day,
That Angel to teach me His ain wondrous way.
For, when sorrow blin's up a' this life to our view,
He aye leaves a place for His han' to come through;
Sae oor wee graves, we ken, are gowd links nocht can dim
Slippit into the chain that leads upward to Him.

TO A CITY FRIEND.

YOU prate about your busy town,
   And look upon myself with pity,
As something too much overgrown
   To grace your cultivated city.
You think me rough and crude as yet,
   Of dwarf'd and undeveloped stature,
And hint the city's wear and fret
   Can tone one down to smoother nature.

I hear you speak without a qualm,
    And soundly rate my village dulness,
But, bless you! I'm not Charles Lamb,
    To weep at all your city's fulness;
I like the street as well as you,
    With all its short, firm, certain paces,
But still one tires to have for view
    An endless magic slide of faces.

But here I sit beside my books,
    Sole hermit of the teeming quiet,
And put on very solemn looks,
    When some stray thought comes out with "fiat;"
The sunbeams from the setting sun
    Come through the window softly peeping,
As if they said, "You're all alone,
    Old fellow, we have caught you sleeping."

From here I wander out at will,
    In wild Bohemian flights of fancies,
Or gather with a simple skill
    New rhymes when in poetic trances.
A very modest Timon, I
    Look back upon your teeming city,
And proffer you, with half a sigh,
    A share of what you give me—pity.

Within the town you cannot get
    A single moment for reflection,
Or wipe from off your brow the sweat
    That's apt to spoil a fair complexion;
But just a jostle, strain, and strive
    To reach a large result in money:
Ach himmel! but your human hive
    Sends into market bitter honey.

"The human tide that sweeps along,"
    (I quote this passage from your letter),
"Can stir the pulses till they throng,
    And start those thoughts that make one better.
For here we have our fellow-men
    Epitomised, and all the labour
Of hand and tool and thought and pen
    Brought out, and ranking with its neighbour.

What high impulses work with me,
    When all around I hear the sighing
And moaning of the human sea,
    As to some greater voice replying.
I stride in front as if to bend
    The tumult back that still will cumber,
And wishing that my village friend
    Were with me to shake off his slumber."

Well, well; you have your streets which lead
    To all the world, so Schiller tells us;
But this truth has no earthly need
    To make me follow Paracelsus.
I watch them from afar, nor dim
    My brain by vague philosophising,
Nor wish to take a plunge, like him,
    For friends to wait and see me rising.

But come and spend a day with me,
    And I shall lay aside the shovel,
And argue with you till I'be
    Like Gil Blas in Le Sage's novel—
Or we shall take a gentler task,
    And lie, half dreaming in the hollows,
And hear, as in the sun we bask,
    Some distant engine playing solos.

Or books. What say you to an hour
    Of Tennyson, or uncouth Browning,
Or naughty Swinburne's rampant power
    That keeps this straight-laced decade frowning?
Or, better still, if you will come,
    We'll read together, just to tease you,
Molière's "*Le Bourgeois gentilhomme*,"
    And I shall be Jourdain to please you.

I lean back and I fix my eye
    Serenely on the airy distance,
You rise, and, waiting for reply,
    You shake your head with dumb persistence.
You city limpet, keep your streets
    That spoil some acres of good tillage,
And I shall sip my rural sweets,
    And eat my lotus in the village.

But *scherz bei seite*, all this talk
    Which round your sportive letter rallies,
Is but mere jokes I like to crack,
    And must be ta'en *cum grano salis*.
I like the town as well as you,
    And when my blood gets dull and thicken'd
I yearn for one wild scamper through
    Its streets to get its current quicken'd.

And what just now with books and rhyme
    I feel I need some slight renewing,
So I must snatch a little time
    To see what all my kind are doing.
Per Bacco, here I toss about
    My books that breed such fret and sorrow,
And so, *du guter mensch*, look out,
    For I shall be in town to-morrow.

MAY MIDDLETON'S TAM.

FRAE the schulehoose that sat at the heid o' the green,
To the fit o' the toon where the smiddy was seen—
Frae the narrow close mooth to the hoose on the brae,
Where the weans at odd times met to scamper an' play—
Frae the heid o' the parish to a' the laigh boun',
In a word, tak' at ance the hale country-side roun',
Frae the laird to the joiner that cooper'd a train,
A' had an ill word o' May Middleton's Tam.

He had gleg een, an' mooth that was aye on the gape,
But his face for sax months hadna lookit on saip;
An' Nature hersel' had supplied him wi' shoon,
Sae waukit he'd dee maist afore they wore dune.
His knees play'd bo-keek through a rive in his breeks,
For his mither lang syne had lost a' faith in steeks;
But he scamper'd aboot fu' o' glee as a lamb—
'Od, an awfu' ill plague was May Middleton's Tam.

The back o' his han' was as broon as a taid,
An', as he had grown since his jacket was made,
The half o' his airm to the elbow was bare,
An' a scrimpit bit sark half in tatters was there;
While, what wi' the dichtin' his nose noo and thaun,
The tae sleeve was bricht as the lid o' a can—
There was nae washin' day to mak' dirt tak' a dwam,
But wear on an' wear dune wi' May Middleton's Tam.

Had a stane been sent through ony window within
A mile frae his hoose, or some mischief been dune;
The mooth o' the pump stappit up, or a score,
Or the heid o' a man drawn wi' chalk on the door;

A deuk or a hen gotten deid, or a wean
Knockit into the siver when flowin' wi' rain—
"Wha could hae dune this?" An' the answer aye cam'—
"Deil tak' him, wha else but May Middleton's Tam!"

He stole a' the bools frae the rest o' the weans,
An' pelted the big anes wha fash'd him wi' stanes;
He knockit aff bonnets, he ran ahint gigs,
He climb'd up on cairts, an' he ran alang brigs;
He jaggit the cuddy o' big ragman Jock
Till the croons that it made nearly frichten'd the folk;
An' yet, at the schule, nane could say verse or psalm
Freer aff heart an' tongue than May Middleton's Tam.

He was heid o' a' ill baith at mornin' an' late,
Sae that maist o' the folk wish'd him oot o' the gate,
But Birky, the maister, wha keepit the schule,
Said, aye when they ca'd him a rascal an' fule—
"There is something in Tam, if ye just wait a wee,
That will mak' ye a' glower, ill an' a' though he be."
But I wat Birky's faith was consider'd a sham,
For the deevil's ain bird was May Middleton's Tam.

He was twice carried hame wi' a cut in his heid,
Ony ithers but him 'twad hae streckit them deid;
But the eggs o' a corbie or piat to him
Were something worth while to risk life for an' limb.
He was catch'd by the miller gaun doon the mill race,
A' the hairm was a fricht, an' less dirt on the face;
An' thrice he was brocht half-droon'd oot o' the dam—
'Od, the hangman was sure o' May Middleton's Tam.

His mither, puir woman, did a' that she could
To keep him in boun's, as a richt mither should;

But ance ower the door, she was oot o' his thocht,
An' a crony gaun by he was ready for ocht.
Then bare-leggit weans at the door micht look oot
To get, in the by-gaun, a push or a cloot;
But they took to their heels wi' a jump like a ram—
They a' stood in fear o' May Middleton's Tam.

But ill as he was, he grew up stoot an' steive,
Braid shuider'd, big baned, an' a dawd o' a neive;
Then he wrocht noo an' thaun, when the simmer cam' roun',
Howin' turnips, or drivin' some nowte to the toon;
But as yet wark an' him werena like to agree,
A' his talk was 'boot sailors an' storms at the sea,
Till ae day he left withoot tears or a qualm,
An' the village was rid o' May Middleton's Tam.

Years gaed by, an' nae word cam' frae Tam, till at last
His mither hersel' thocht that a' hope was past,
When ae day the postman gaed in at the door—
A thing the douce neebours had ne'er ken'd afore;
But aye after that a blin' man micht hae seen
That her hoose an' hersel' were mair cheerfu' an' bien.
"Lod," quo' ane, as she lean'd hersel' 'gainst the door jamb,
"Has ocht been sent hame by her ne'er-dae-weel Tam?"

But a greater surprise they were a' yet to get,
When the handy bit farm o' Whaupfields was to let;
Neebours ran into neebours wi' weans in their arm,
Cryin', "Help us, May Middleton's Tam's got the farm;"
An' after awee, it was heard Tam himsel'
Wad be back in his ain native clachan to dwell.
He cam', an' the doors were as fu' as could cram
Wi' folk keen to look at May Middleton's Tam.

But losh! what a braw, strappin' fellow they saw,
Broon-faced, and a beard that was black as a craw;
Lang, lang did they glower, till the blacksmith said " Fegs,
What a change since he broke wi' a stane Whaupey's legs."
Here it cam' to his min' o' the wark on the farm,
Sae he added, " But Tam never did ony harm."
Then he ended by makin' a sort o' salaam
Doon the street to the hoose o' May Middleton's Tam.

But when ance Tam was into his farm, an' had made
A' things snod, an' his mither as mistress array'd,
He tea'd a' the neebors, and tellt them what wark
He had makin' a fortune that cost him much cark.
Then he turn'd roun' to Birky, the maister, wha sat
By his side, lookin' up as if prood aboot that,
An' said, clappin' his back, " Here's your health in a dram,
For ye aye took the pairt o' May Middleton's Tam."

An' frae that day to this ilka body speaks weel
O' Tam, while they praise his guid praties an' meal;
An' mithers, wha ance could hae seen his neck thrawn,
Gie him days at the hay when there's ower muckle mawn.
E'en the landlord himsel' comes an' cries, unco big,
" Here, boy, come an' haud Mr Middleton's gig."
For since things took a turn, an' his guid fortune cam',
He is noo nae mair ken'd as May Middleton's Tam.

DAFT AILIE.

DAFT Ailie cam' in by the auld brig-en'
  As the sunlicht, saft an' sweet,
Fell doon on the laigh, white wa's o' the toon,
  An' the lang, quate, single street.

It fell on her sair-worn, wrinkled face,
  An' on her thin gray hair;
But the licht that lay in her een was a licht
  That shouldna hae been there.

An' aye she lookit roun' an' roun',
  An' aye a waefu' smile
Lay on her lips, that were thin an' white,
  As she mum'led an' sang the while.

Then the weans cam' rinnin' oot o' the schule—
  The schule had scaled for the nicht—
An' they a' cam' roun' Daft Ailie, an' cried
  An' laup in their mad delicht.

Then they took a haud o' each ither's han's,
  And made her gang in the ring,
An' they danced roun' aboot her, an' sang a sang
  That made the hooses ring.

But when they had danced an' jamp their fill,
  They closer an' closer drew,
Cryin', "Ailie, afore we let you oot,
  Ye maun make us a bonnie boo."

Then she boo'd to them a' as they stood aroun',
　　Wi' the boo o' a leddy born,
An' said, " O, weanies, baith ane an' a',
　　Ye maun come to my bridal the morn.

But I maun away to the auld wud brig,
　　An' sit 'neath the rowan tree,
An' there I will wait till my bonnie bridegroom
　　Comes ower to marry me."

" An' what is your bonnie bridegroom like,
　　Is he strong, an' braid, an' braw ?
An' wha is he that will come an' tak'
　　Auld Ailie frae us a' ?"

" Oh, my ain bridegroom is tall an' fair,
　　An' straucht as a hazel tree,
An' licht is the touch o' his han' in mine,
　　When he speaks in the gloamin' to me.

An' weel he likes me, I ken, an' weel
　　Can he whisper his manly voo ;
An' weel I like to listen to him—
　　I can hear his voice the noo.

I saw ane laid oot in white deid-claes,
　　But my een were unco dim,
An' I couldna hear a word that was said,
　　Though they tauld me it was him.

But I turn'd my heid frae the cauld, white deid,
　　That was quate as quate could be,
An' turn'd an' gaed doon to the brig, to wait
　　For my bridegroom comin' to me.

But I sometimes think he is unco lang,
    An' I weary a' the day,
Waitin' here for my bonnie bridegroom to come
    An' tak his Ailie away."

"But, Ailie, Ailie," the weans cry out,
    "Your hair is grey an' thin,
An' your cheeks are sae sunk that nae bonnie bridegroom
    Will come sic a bride to win."

"O, weanies, weanies! haud a' your tongues;
    Ye dinna ken what ye say;
My cheek is reid, an' my e'e is bricht,
    For I'm twenty-ane this day.

But I maun away to the auld wud brig,
    An' sit 'neath the rowan tree;
Dinna gang to the schule the morn, but come
    An' see my bridegroom an' me."

Then they let her oot o' the ring, an' she gangs
    Wi' the same strange, waefu' smile,
Doon the lang quate street, an' she sings a sang
    As they follow her a' the while.

But she hauds her way to the en' o' the toon,
    An' aye she sorts her hair,
Wi' the same wild licht flaffin' up in her een
    That shouldna hae been there.

O, weans! O, weans! gang a' to your hames,
    An' let puir Ailie alane;
She gangs to sit by the auld wud brig
    To settle her wan'erin' brain.

DAFT AILIE.

She sits for hoors by that auld, frail brig,
   Ow'r the braid, deep, dookin' pool,
But a weary, weary wait she will hae,
   As she sings her sangs o' dool;

For nae bonnie bridegroom will ever come
   To tak' her by the han',
Save ane that comes frae the lan' o' the deid,
   When the last lang breath is drawn.

But weel I min' that, in a' the toon,
   The brawest amang them a'
Was Ailie, wha noo gangs frae hoose to hoose,
   Giein' ilka body a ca'.

Her cheeks had the saft, sweet bloom o' youth,
   An' gowden her lang, thick hair,
An' bricht was the look o' her bonnie blue e'e,
   For a sweet life-dream was there.

Ay, weel micht they glance like the simmer licht,
   When the sun gangs doon in the west,
For the first pure dream o' love was there,
   And it wadna gie her rest.

But her bridal day cam' quickly roun',
   An' mirth an' daffin' was rife,
As we sat ben the room for the hoor to come
   That wad see sweet Ailie a wife.

An' O! but she lookit bonnie an' braw
   In the flush o' her maiden pride;
An' should I live to a hunner lang years,
   I shall ne'er see a bonnier bride.

But waes me! whaten a storm cam' on
    On that happy afternoon;
The Nith rase up wi' an angry sough,
    An' reid wi' wrath cam' doon.

The nicht drappit doon, and it grew sae dark
    That the hill abune the brae,
Where ye gather in simmer the berries sae black,
    Was hid as if ta'en away.

An' never a single star was seen
    In the heaven sae dark an' wide,
Yet lichtly the bridegroom cam' doon the path,
    To claim his winsome bride.

The lave that were wi' him they talkit an' lauch'd
    In a' their youth an' glee,
Till they cam' to the brig ow'r the dookin' pool,
    By the lang, braid rowan tree.

Then the young gudeman that was soon to be
    Gaed on't wi' a lichtsome spang;
An' he cried to the lave to come on behin',
    For Ailie wad think them lang.

But alake! what a cry gaed up through the nicht,
    To the heicht o' the stars aboon—
Sic a cry never rase to their flickerin' licht
    Save frae lips o' men that droon.

For half o' the brig had been torn away
    By the angry strength o' the spate,
An' the young bridegroom slippit ow'r in the dark
    To his quick an' awfu' fate.

They faun' him next day in the minister's holm,
    Where the water had flung him oot;
An' they brocht him up to the far toon-en',
    But they happit his bridal suit.

They laid him doon, an' they took it aff,
    An' dress'd him frae heid to feet
In the dress they pit on when we're wedded to death—
    The lang, white windin' sheet.

Then Ailie cam' in, but O, what a change
    Had come on her through the nicht;
Her gowden hair had a scance o' gray,
    An' her een had a strange wild licht.

An' aye she lookit, an' turn'd roun' an' roun',
    While they watch'd her a' the while;
"O, where is my bonnie bridegroom?" she ask'd,
    An' her lips had a waefu' smile.

"O, Ailie, this is your bonnie bridegroom
    That lies in the airms o' death;
Will ye no tak' a look at his face, an' kiss
    The lips that hae nae breath?"

"O haud your tongues, haud a' your tongues,
    Dinna tell sic lees to me;
I will gang mysel' to the auld wud brig,
    My ain bridegroom to see.

I will wait by the rowan tree till he comes—
    I ken that he winna be late,
An' I'll sing the sangs I hae heard him sing,
    They will cheer me as I wait."

So she turn'd an' gaed doon to the auld wud brig,
    As ye see her gang the noo,
Wi' the same waefu' smile on her thin white lips,
    An' the sorrow upon her broo.

An' aye she wan'ers aboot the brig,
    Ye may see her late an' sune,
Still waitin' for him wha is in his grave,
    An' the green, green grass abune.

Then, weanies, weanies, gang a' to your hames,
    An' let puir Ailie be;
Ye little ken what a weird she drees,
    By the auld braid rowan tree.

A' HIS LANE.

PIT his back against a chair,
    Let us see if he can gang,
But be ready wi' your han'
    If he sways or ocht gaes wrang;
Mammy wadna like to see
    Ony ill come to her wean;
There noo, leave him to himsel',
    Mammy's bairnie's a' his lane.

What a thrawin' o' his mou',
    What a rowin' o' his een,
Then a steady look at me,
    An' the space that lies between;

Noo, ae fittie's oot a bit,
  Look at him, he's unco fain,
Straicht himsel' up like a man,
  Mammy's bairnie's a' his lane.

There, he's left the chair at last,
  Lauchin' in his merry glee—
Haudin' oot a wee, plump han',
  As if to say, "Tak' haud o' me."
Juist anither step, an' then—
  Gudesake, what a thraw he's ta'en!
There, he's fairly ow'r at last—
  Coupit when he's left his lane.

Did he hurt his curly heid?
  Let his mammy clap the place,
Pay the stule, an' kiss his croon
  Till the tears are aff his face.
There noo; lean him to the chair—
  Let us try the bairn again;
Half-a-dozen fa's are nocht,
  If he learns to gang his lane.

Steady this time wi' his feet—
  Dinna keep his legs sae wide.
See, I hae my han' to kep
  If he sways to ony side.
Mercy! what a solemn face
  Lookin' up to meet my ain;
There, he's in my lap at last;
  Here's a bairn can gang his lane.

Mither life has unco wark,
  Settin' up her weans to gang;

Some pit oot ae fit, then stop,
   Ithers step oot an' fa' wrang;
Very few can keep their feet
   As they stot ow'r clod or stane;
Angels greet abune to see
   Hoo we fa' when left oor lane.

THE SAN' MAN.

SAN' man frae the quarry hole,
   Bring a pouk o' san';
Stan' ahint my back, an' tak'
   A neivefu' in your han'.
Here's a fechtin', restless wean,
   To every mischief gi'en;
Fling a handfu' in his face,
   And gar him rub his een.

I hae done what mithers may
   To please this glow'rin' fule—
Made a stable for his horse
   By turnin' up the stule;
Tied the cart-string roun' its neck—
   I did the same yestreen—
Yet he rocks and coonts his taes,
   An' winna rub his een.

I hae sat frae six to eicht,
   This rogue upon my knee;
I may sit anither hoor,
   For onything I see.

THE SAN' MAN.

No a sign o' sleep ava,
    What can a' this mean?
San' man frae the quarry hole,
    Come an' fill his een.

Ben he comes wi' lang slow steps,
    Seen an' heard by nane,
Hauds a gowpenfu' o' san'
    Richt aboon the wean.
Drap, drap, the san' rins doon,
    Through fingers lang an' lean;
San' man, tak' away your han',
    See, he rubs his een.

What a rubbin' wi' his neive,
    Row'd as if to fecht;
What a raxin' oot o' legs,
    Then an unco weicht.
Soun' at last, although he focht
    Wi' a' his micht an' main—
Ready wi' his creddly ba',
    Here's a sleepin' wean.

In this restless age o' oors,
    Seam'd wi' speirin' doot,
Mony a san' man ane could name
    Stogs an' slings aboot.
We, wha are but bearded weans,
    Wunner what they mean,
When they fling their creeds aboot,
    An' gar us rub oor een.

RID OF HIS ENGINE.

THE way that it came about was this—
   I was stoker for over two years to Bill,
But something was always going amiss
   With that creaking confounded engine still.

We never ran time, and were always late;
   Now a throttle valve would get choked and stop,
Then an axle grow hot as a coal in the grate,
   Next a tube would burst and—into the shop.

How Bill did swear when delays took place,
   He would chew till his lips were almost black,
Then say, with an oath, looking into my face—
   "I wish I was rid of this engine, Jack."

But she stuck to us still, like one of the Fates,
   Snorting and creaking on until
A sort of a proverb grew up with our mates,
   "Six hours behind time, like Jack and Bill."

Well, one night on our way through Deepside Moss—
   It was then our turn out with the midnight goods—
Bill had sworn at the engine till he was cross,
   And had now sunk into his sleepy moods.

When, just as I lifted up my head
   From the furnace door, there right in front
(I had miss'd the signal standing red),
   Was a mineral train that had stopp'd to shunt.

I shut off the steam, and I shook up Bill—
"For God's sake look out"—when with one wild roar,
And a crash that is making my ears ring still,
We pitch'd into the train, and I knew no more.

When I came to myself I was down the bank,
Half a yard from my head lay a waggon wheel,
With its axle twisted and bent like a crank,
But no hurt was upon me that I could feel.

Then I heard coming downward the sound of speech,
And struggling up to the top, I found
That engine and tender lay piled on each,
With a fencework of waggons and vans around.

"What a smash!" said the guard, and I ask'd "Where's Bill?"
He turn'd, and the light of his lamp was cast
On a form at my feet, lying stiff and still :
Bill had got rid of his engine at last.

LOOK TO THE EAST.

THE dead man came from out the grave,
    He grasp'd my hand, and said, " Be brave."

I cried, " So very far away,
    Yet thou hast sympathy with clay."

He said, " What would it profit me
    To turn from thy humanity ?"

"Alas!" I sigh'd, "I am but dust,
And the old failing of mistrust

Comes up within me, and I fear
I falter with no purpose here."

The dead man stood like one who saith
A prayer, then ask'd, "Hast thou no faith?"

I look'd at him; within his eyes
The tears rose up as in surprise.

Then I made answer to his thought—
"Thou knowest all, and I know naught."

Across his brow a shade of pain
Pass'd, but to leave it clear again.

He ask'd, reproach his voice within,
"Art thou, too, smitten with that sin

Which looks before this life, to seek
What God himself will never speak,

Until this death we paint so grim,
Guide thee through the dread grave to Him?"

I bow'd my head as if in shame
To hear the dead man's gentle blame.

Then, sweet and low, he spoke again,
"Hast thou faith in thy fellow-men?"

"Yea," I return'd, "for still my kind
Toil to leave something good behind,

Which, in the unborn after years,
Will ripen kindly with their peers."

I paused, and he, when this was said,
Laid one soft hand upon my head,

And thus made answer ere I wist,
" Behind thy kind work God and Christ,

And all the marvels men can do,
Are but the shadow of these Two.

Whom, then, deserves thy greater trust,
God, Christ, or men who are but dust?"

I knelt down at the dead man's feet;
His tears fell on me soft and sweet.

He raised me up, and hand in hand
We stood, as two together stand.

Then breast to breast, within my ear
He whisper'd words of love and cheer.

Such words a living mortal may
Not whisper, but the dead can say.

Then said, as he touch'd lips and eyes,
" Look to the east; the sun will rise."

I turn'd; my soul was strong again
To trust God, Christ, and toiling men.

And still when doubt wakes from its rest
That dead man clasps me to his breast,

And soul to soul like friends respond :
Mine from this earth ; his from beyond.

Mine sighs, " I falter ;" his replies,
" Look to the east; the sun will rise."

JOHN KEATS.

*" He is made one with Nature; there is heard
His voice in all her music."—Shelley.*

THERE be more things within that far-off breast,
    Whereon the flowers grow,
Of the boy poet, in his Roman rest,
    Than hearts like ours can know.

He slumbers, but his sleep hath not our fears,
    For all aside is thrown ;
And from the gateway of his tombèd years
    A power is moving on.

And in that power is hid a voice that speaks
    To hearts that throb and rise
From common earth, and worship that which seeks
    The wider sympathies.

For he is silent not ; and from the bounds
    Wherein his footsteps move
Come, like the wind at morn, all summer sounds
    Of boyhood thought and love.

So he to us is as an oracle
　Whose words bedrip with youth;
The latest spirit, bathing in the well
　Of Pagan shape and truth.

A passionate existence which we scan;
　But first must lay aside
The rougher thinking that belongs to man,
　And take the unsettled pride

Of eager youth and fancy, and a strength
　Misled by the fond zeal
For Grecian look and light, yet found at length
　The power to touch and feel.

So, taking this into thy thought, ye trace
　His wealth of opening lore;
He bursts upon you with his freshest grace,
　And moves a man no more—

But a bright shadow in the heart's expanse
　Crown'd with the tenderest rays
Of love, and thought of as the far-off glance
　Of early summer days.

So bring him from beneath the sky of Rome,
　From all her youngest flowers.
I weep that there his dust should find a home,
　And all his spirit ours!

But no! ye cannot; for a bond he keeps
　Whose ties are firmly strung—
The lone yet passionate heart of Shelley sleeps
　Beside the dust he sung.

And it were vain to leave him there and foil
    His rest—so let them sleep
Within the silence of that glorious soil,
    Whose inspirations steep

Their songs in colours like the summer boughs,
    Whose freshness ever strives,
And blooms, like asphodels, upon the brows
    Of two immortal lives.

And there they sleep, as if their fates had said
    They shall not sleep alone;
The singer and the sung must fill one bed,
    And make their ashes one.

And so it is; and through the years that roll,
    That sepulchre of theirs
Is as a passionate and wish'd-for goal
    To which all thought repairs—

While in our hearts, as is their dust at Rome,
    Their spirits feel no wrong;
But shine to us like gods serenely from
    The Pantheon of Song.

THE QUESTIONING ANGELS.

THERE ran behind the angels' wings
    An undertone of murmurings,

Faint, as when sighing autumn grieves,
And wrings her palms of wither'd leaves.

Then God said, as He heard the sound,
"Who murmurs?" And He look'd around.

But never folded pinion stirr'd,
Or lip to speak one single word.

Such silence in the heavens dwelt,
The motions of the stars were felt.

"Who murmurs here?" He ask'd again,
With something on His brow like pain.

At length one trembling angel said,
With bending knee and bowing head:

"We murmur, for we cannot see
The earth as it appears to Thee.

We look, and only see below
An endless stretch of human woe."

Then God touch'd with his finger-tips,
While sunshine clad His brow and lips,

The doubting angels' eyes, that could
See naught on earth that seem'd of good.

"Look now," He said, "and what ye see
Turn round, and straightway tell to me."

They look'd; one angel from his place
Made answer, looking in His face:

"Father, thine own great purpose runs
Round men, as planets round their suns,

And binds them like a golden band,
The end of which is in Thy hand,

For some great good we cannot see,
Yet rooted and full-growth'd in Thee.

We murmur not; this much we know,
Thy shadow falls on men below.

And all, when truly understood,
Is fair and wise, and pure and good."

He who can stand upon the earth,
And see all things take perfect birth,

The same hath felt in awed surprise
God's fingers laid upon his eyes.

JIM'S WHISTLE.

NO, the railway wasn't a fitting place
    For a man like him, at least one in his case;
But though deaf and dumb, he was quick of the eye,
And was first to warn when a train came nigh.
Why, instead of keeping our eye on Jim,
We came in our turn to be watch'd by him.

Whether it was express going past,
Special, mineral, goods, slow or fast,
It was all the same. Jim could always catch
Up and down line, as if set to watch.

JIM'S WHISTLE.

When we heard his cry, short, sharp, and clear,
"Jim's Whistle," we said, and at once stood clear.

Clever workman he was, and handy, too;
Knew at a glance what he had to do;
He was my mate, and 'twas something to see
The finger talk between him and me,
And to hear him laugh to the rest of our mates
When he tried to tickle me over the plates.

At our dinner hour, when we sat at the side
Of the cutting, Jim took a sort of pride
In sitting near me, while his fingers said
All the quaint, strange thoughts that came into his head;
While at each he would laugh, till the rest would say,
"Jim's in one of his talking moods to-day."

But I lost him at last: though my mate for years,
And quick of the eye, I had still my fears
That Jim would get snapp'd in spite of our pains,
By engine and tender or passing trains.
And it came at last so sudden and quick,
We left in the four-feet shovel and pick:

'Twas in Dixon's cut. Jim had been that day
Full of finger talk in his own swift way,
When, just as we clear'd the down line for a train
That was coming onward with jolt and strain,
Round the curve of the up line, swift as the wind,
Came a passenger train, half-an-hour behind.

A cry from us all and a leap to the side,
As the train tore on with its terrible stride;
But where was Jim? We had miss'd his cry—
The whistle that warn'd when a train was nigh.

Alas! in the six-feet, stiff of limb,
With the blood on his face and lips lay—Jim.

I ran to his side and lifted his head,
One look was enough—my mate was dead;
I laid him down in the self-same place,
Then turn'd away with the tears on my face.
"Jim's Whistle," said one, that was all our speech,
As we stood in our grief looking each at each.

And now at my daily work, other mate
Than Jim on the other side of the plate,
I sometimes start with the wish to cry,
"Jim's Whistle, lads, let the train go by."
And often my fingers go up, as if Jim
Were with me, and I were talking to him.

TWO EYES.

TWO eyes, whose light I lost when death
   Came in and took away the breath,
Are with me, and though still unseen
Speak of the past, and what has been.
They shine upon me night and day
As twin stars in the heaven may.
And when their warmth is in my breast,
All earth-thoughts settle into rest;
But in their stead rise others, which
Take quiet voice, and wisdom preach.
I hear them, thinking of that voice
Which made the sky its early choice,

And all the music of its tone
But sounds to lead me on and on.
So in calm childlike trust I walk,
A growing reverence in my talk,
Not daring to look up, for fear
Those heaven-lit eyes should disappear.

MOVE UPWARD.

*" Move upward, working out the brute,
And let the ape and tiger die."—Tennyson.*

AY, in heaven's name, let us move upward still
   In this time-changing planet of ours,
And bring to the task what the gods still ask—
   The best of our years and our pow'rs.
Let us make this great century, whirling around,
   A footstool to lift up the foot,
Whereon we may cry, looking upward to God—
   "We are all this way from the brute."

Is the dream of the poet forever to be
   Like the myth of the Greek, or at least
The skeleton dress'd up in costliest gold,
   And set in the midst of the feast ?
Is the double meaning forever to wind
   Like the coil of the snake round our speech ?
And the Dead Sea fable still utter its truth
   As we mimic and chatter to each ?

But questions are weapons an infant can lift,
  Let us marry the fruitfuller act,
And widen our being to let in the light,
  And the strength of the deed-giving fact.
Is it not enough we have come from God?
  But since Time took his birthright in years,
We have bred with the brute, and our offspring has been
  The sucklings of bloodshed and tears.

It were time, then, to burst from the links we have forged
  To fetter the soul in the breast,
Though the wrench should bring with it the best of our blood,
  And we faint as a pilgrim for rest.
Heart! but each has some task he must close with his life
  When he slips from this world's wide plan,
And the highest a man can shape out for himself
  Is to move himself upward to man.

Ay, move himself up to that nature of his
  Which, though trampled and trod in the dust,
Still shows, as a jewel may gleam through the sand,
  The finger of God through its crust.
Let him, then, so alive with miraculous breath,
  Make the best of his energies join,
Till he lift himself up in the light of the Christ
  To the clear, true ring of the coin.

There be some who squat down by the world's rough path,
  As if life were a burden to shirk,
Heeding not the great watchword it thunders to all—
  "Up, shoulder to shoulder, and work!"
But sit in their darkness to wince at the truth,
  As an owl at the light sits and blinks,
And for ever propound each his question to solve,
  Like a nineteenth-century Sphinx.

"Move upward from what ?" they break in, with a croak,
 And I answer at once in reply—
"From the sham that has flung our soul under its heel,
 And the words that are wrap to a lie—
From the thought that still grovels and hides in the dust,
 As a viper may do, until blind
It springs up to find venom to add to its own,
 In the plague-spots seen in our kind.

Ay, battle with this as a fighter strikes out,
 When he stands with his back to the wall,
With no help but the strength that is in his right arm,
 And the eye that has glances for all.
Shame on us, then, who stand with our face to the front,
 And modell'd in God's mighty shape,
If we roughen our soul with the dust of the earth,
 To give better foothold for the ape.

God ! to look on this manifold, wonderful earth,
 As Novalis look'd on men,
And feel the old reverence grow upward within
 To the pitch of the Hebrew's again—
To have the rapt soul and the calm, deep eye
 That can look upon all without fear,
And the firm, steady beat of the heart that can feel
 When the footsteps of God are anear.

It may be that we may, fighting upward to this,
 Grow footsore and faint in the heat,
But the moving oneself up to heights in this life
 Spreads no carpeted way for the feet.
Let us think of those grand, true souls who have left
 Guiding posts on each side of the way,
And press ever on with our eyes to the light
 They have left as a part of their day,

Ay, in Heaven's name, let us move upward, then,
    To the grand, true ring of the man,
Giving to this one task all the best of our years,
    And the strength to reach up to the plan.
Let the "*Ernst ist das Leben*" of Schiller speak on,
    Till we seize and place under our foot
The head of the ape, crying upward to God,
    "Lo! at last we are free from the brute!"

SONG OF THE ENGINE.

IN the shake and rush of the engine,
    In the full, deep breath of his chest,
In the swift, clear clank of the gleaming crank,
    In his soul that is never at rest,
In the spring and ring of the bending rail,
    As he thunders and hurtles along,
A strong world's melody fashions itself,
    And this smoke demon calls it his song.

"Hurrah! for my path I devour in my wrath,
    As I rush to the cities of men
With a load I lay down like a slave at their feet,
    Then turn and come backward again.
Hurrah! for the rush of the yielding air
    That gives way to my wild, fierce springs
As I keep to the rail, while my heart seems to burst
    In a wild, mad craving for wings.

I rush by hills where the shepherds are seen
  Like a speck as they walk on their side;
I roar through glens and by rocks that shake
  As I quicken the speed of my stride.
I glide by woods and by rock-bound streams
  That hurry and race in their glee,
But swift as they run, with their face to the sun,
  They can never keep pace with me.

I tear through caverns of sudden dark,
  Like that in which first I lay,
Ere the cunning of man had alit on a plan
  To drag me up to the day.
I rush with a shriek, which is all I can speak,
  A wild protest against fear;
But I come to the light with a snort of delight,
  And my black breath far in the rear.

I crash along bridges that span the hills,
  And catch at a glimpse below
The roof-thatch'd cot and the low white wall
  Lying white in the sun's last glow.
Or it may be the gleam of some dull, broad stream
  Creeping slowly onward beneath,
While within its breast for a moment I catch
  The shadow and film of my breath.

I rush over roofs in my madness of flight,
  But not like the demon of old;
I leave them unturn'd, for the arches in air
  Bear me up, and my feet keep their hold.
At times, too, I catch, when I check my speed,
  The long, wide lane of the street,
And hear, 'twixt the snorts of my own fierce breath,
  The clamour and hurry of feet.

Then I snatch a look at the puppets beneath,
  But to snort and rush onward again,
With a fear at my heart almost quenching its heat,
  For heavens! these must be men—
Ay, men, I could bend like the willow, but who,
  With a thought that from nothing will shrink,
Have hurl'd me down with their hands on my throat,
  And bound me in rivet and link.

I rush by village, and cottage, and farm;
  I thunder sudden and quick
Upon handfuls of men who leap out of my way,
  And lean on their shovel and pick.
There is one brown fellow among them who sings
  The terrible sweep of my limb;
The fool! dare he mimic this music of mine,
  And such pitiful music in him?

I flare through the night when the stars are bright,
  With the lights of the city for mark;
With bound upon bound I shake the ground,
  As I feel for the rail in the dark.
And I know that the stars whisper each to each,
  As downward they flicker and peer,
'What is this that these fellows have hit on below,
  That seems like a meteor from here?'

For my great eye glistens and gleams in the front,
  As if to give light to my tread,
While behind like the fires of a Vulcan flung out,
  Three others glare thirsty and red.
And the flame licking round the fierce life in my heart,
  Let loose for a moment upsprings,
And darts through the whirls of my breath overhead,
  Till it makes me a demon with wings.

I send through the city's wild heart shocks of life,
  But to feel them come back like a wave ;
I loom broad and swart in wild traffic's rough mart,
  I kneel to men like a slave.
I gather from all the four ends of the earth,
  What profit and use there may be—
Did the Greek ever dream, in his talk with the gods,
  Of a wild beast of burden like me ?

But often my own wild thoughts leap far ahead,
  And I question myself with a moan—
' Will I ripen and grow into sinew and limb
  With the higher race that comes on ?
Or shall I grow white with the hour of the years
  That, falling, cankers and wears—
Turning feeble of limb with the things that benumb,
  And steal the vigour from theirs ?

Were this worthy end for a being like mine,
  Begot in the frenzy of thought,
And sent as the type of the soul of this age,
  Setting time and distance at nought ?
No, if there be death, let it come in the end,
  For my iron-girt bosom will beat,
Till the judgment-bolts flung from the right hand of God
  Smite the pathway from under my feet.' "

Thus he snorts and sings as he thunders by me,
  This wild smoke-demon of ours,
While from end to end the rail quivers and bends
  To his thousand Hercules' powers.
And his great breath mixes and whirls with the clouds,
  While he whoops as if mad with glee :
" Did the Greek ever dream in his talk with the gods
  Of a black beast of burden like me ?"

THE SINGERS.

GOD said, "I will reach my hand down to earth,
That man may have in him a purer birth;

For the melody hidden within his breast,
For want of a singer, is dead to the rest.

But he whom I touch shall at once have power
To open his lips with a singing dower;

And, spreading his melody far and free,
Men shall turn and listen and think of me."

Then He reach'd His hand to the earth, and lo!
Like woodland buds when the spring winds blow;

So the hearts He touch'd rose up and grew strong
With an unseen strength, which took shape in song!

They sung in the city, where the long street
Was one great echo of human feet;

They sung in lanes where the shadows lay still;
They sung in glen and on breezy hill;

And the hearts of the angels were strangely stirr'd,
When the melodies of the earth were heard.

For within them there ran a sweet undertone
Of the music that God set apart as their own.

Then they question'd their Master, and said, "We hear
Stray notes of our melody floating near;

But far above them swell other sounds,
That burst their own and celestial bounds.

Why is it that one with the same full breast
Can sing till his song overshadows the rest?"

Then God said, "He of the lowly band
Who sings, I have touch'd him with my hand;

But he whose song to thine own is wed
Sings with my hand laid upon his head."

GOD WRAPT HIM.

GOD wrapt him in a world of purer light
   And clearer thought. His soul
Pulsed into being, gifted with far might.
      The roll

Of inner melodies was his to sing,
   And teach its power to men.
His words, like the full breath of virgin Spring,
      Again

Shook drops of noble life upon the heart
   Waiting for such, which beat,
At the high cunning of his rhythmic art,
      In heat

Of music. Pealing to all ends of earth,
    The God-given mighty sound
Rose up, and brought with it a purer birth,
        Whose bound

Was from the earth to heaven. As he sang,
    In high, rapt moods, he threw
Strange utterances that fell without a clang,
        Like dew

On hearts of men, who, feeling their soul stirr'd
    Far down within, from dim
Thoughts, question'd "If the power was in the word,
        Or him?"

They struck strange Memnons, getting vain replies,
    And vainer sounds, but still
They ask'd the foolish and the seeming wise
        What will

Bore him thus up to catch the inward tones
    That light as cloudlets float
So far above in heaven's star-gemm'd zones
        Remote.

At length they came upon one man who stood
    Rapt in his thought, alone,
Around him all the deep, forecasting mood
        Was thrown.

He said, "The poet fathoms, as he sings,
    With eye and heart, the high
Pure influences of supernal things,
        Which fly

From earth to heaven. He, as on a chord
 That some deft finger plays,
Touches the heart and lip with many a word,
 That strays,

Making fair melody, as on it floats
 In shapeless flight, till those
Who listen hear God's co-eternal thoughts
 Disclose

Their meaning in its music, as a tone
 Which one may hear, at first
Starting from low beginnings, rolling on
 To burst

In far reverberations, echoing
 In climaxes along,
Till, as with one broad, universal wing
 The strong

Eternal harmony still rising up
 To join with heaven, but seems
The veilèd Beautiful, with golden cup,
 Whose streams

Forever flowing cool hot hearts and lips
 Of eager men, until
They feel the half of God's apocalypse.
 The skill

By which the poet, standing among men,
 One of themselves, works this,
Is caught from God, but to go back again,
 For His

GOD WRAPT HIM.

Are all the melodies, from the far spheres
   Down to the lowest winds
That open unseen lips when twilight nears.
      Men's minds

Glow at such manifold tones, and rising higher
   To purer heights they feel
The omnific splendours of the poet's fire
      Reveal

The everlasting good framed out for men,
   And all the cross and dim
Great world grows clearer, lifting up again
      To Him

Who made it all its thousand hands of prayer,
   By solemn night and day,
As if great angels with their harps were there
      Alway.

Thus the high poet, feeling all his art,
   In stirless calm, repeats
That breathing which, from God's own leaping heart,
      Completes

All systems that have in eternal space
   Their starr'd and blue abodes:
He grasps their music, standing with his face
      To God's.

THE OPEN SECRET.

GOD said, "I take my stand behind
Men, Nature, and the shaping mind.

And cry, 'The open secret lies
To him who reads with proper eyes.'"

Then thought came boldly forth, and lent
Its strength to conquer what was meant.

The Hebrew with his passionate heart
Came on, and solved it part by part.

The high Greek saw, but turn'd aside,
With beauty walking by his side.

At last came One, upon whose head
The light of God Himself was shed.

He read the secret, and divine
Forever after grew each line.

Then sullen cycles follow'd Him,
In which His reading would not dim.

The ages sped, but still took heed
To wait, and mould a band at need.

Whose worded cunning might lay bare
The omnific secret everywhere.

Stern Dante saw it, though his face,
Was darken'd by the nether place.

Next Shakespeare, who, before his kind,
Stept with it forming in his mind.

Then Milton, blind and old in years,
Stood nearer to it than his peers.

Later a Goethe wander'd by,
To see it only with his eye.

At last the nineteenth century came,
With railway track and furnace flame,

At which, as at a mighty need,
Men's thoughts flew into headlong speed.

Then one rose up, whose northern ire
Smote shams, like sudden bursts of fire.

A roughly-block'd Apollo, strong
To pierce the coiling Python, Wrong.

Last, Science, waking from her sleep,
Sent forth her thought to sound the deep,

But, like the dove sent from the ark,
It came back, having found no mark.

Then she stood up and proudly said,
"The open secret is not read."

O foolish one! Wrap weeds of shame
Around that keen device you claim.

"Behold!" cries God, "I stand and teach,
The open secret is for each.

I slip my own wide soul behind
Men, nature, and the shaping mind,

And he who can unite these three,
Until they lose themselves in me,

The same hath in him, night and day,
The open secret I display."

BY THE SAME AUTHOR,

"A SONG OF LABOUR, AND OTHER POEMS."

OPINIONS OF THE PRESS.

George Gilfillan, Dundee.—Here is verily a "sign of the times"—a perfect phenomenon—a volume of true poetry, testifying to a powerful and, most astonishing of all, a well-cultivated mind, by a working railway navvy or surfaceman on the Glasgow and South-Western Railway. The Ayrshire ploughman, or the Edinburgh barber, the Glasgow pattern drawer, the Paisley weaver, the Clydesdale miner, the Aberdeen policeman, are scarcely so wonderful as the Kirkconnel surfaceman. . . . . . The sons of toil will rejoice to hear the ring and rattle of their work returned on them in poetry and music, and will hail him as their representative, the true "Railway King."

People's Friend.—This writer, who assumes that name (Surfaceman), shows a refinement of language, a culture of intellect, a nobility of mind and heart, and a command of language and imagery astonishing even where the highest training has been received in College halls and classes. And yet, nevertheless, Mr Anderson has been, and is at this present moment, a surfaceman, working on the Glasgow and South-Western Railway—a "common navvy," as he not unfrequently designates himself—with pick and shovel toiling for his daily bread.

Scotsman.—What will remain the most remarkable in this volume is the rare degree of culture to which this Railway Surfaceman has attained; for not only has he made himself so familiar as to be able to use it with care and effect in his own poems, but he is apparently familiar with German literature, talking glibly of Schiller and Goethe, and prefixing to several pieces German quotations, which we presume him able to translate, and also shows an acquaintance with French in his translation of "Hope and Sleep" from Voltaire.

Athenæum.—They (the poems) show a remarkable power in the author of assimilating what he reads, and of expressing his own thoughts with vigour and poetical taste.

Liverpool Daily Albion.—This is a very remarkable book, and Mr Anderson is evidently a very remarkable man.

The Railway News and Joint-Stock Journal.—There is a true ring of poetry in the book, and it may be a subject of pride to sixteen thousand platelayers engaged on the railways of the United Kingdom to have such a poet in their

OPINIONS OF THE PRESS—CONTINUED.

Glasgow Herald.—His efforts in Scotch are almost uniformly good; one or two of the sonnets are capital; and the volume, as a whole, may be taken as a proof that the author will yet produce something of higher mark.

Glasgow News.—This volume will no doubt at once become a favourite, and please and soothe many a heart in the fortunes of homely life; and, if we mistake not, it will receive a cordial welcome from the press in all quarters.

Ayr Observer.—An educated *surfaceman*, a polished and gentle-minded wielder of hammer, pick and shovel, is truly a *rara avis in terra;* but it is out of just such incongruous surroundings, and these, too, intensified by distance from any particular centre of culture, that there has sprung as remarkable a producer of verse as any that our century has seen. . . . A rough-handed son of toil, who is likely to make his neighbourhood a notable one in future years.

Aberdeen Journal.—The author possesses genuine poetic power, not of the highest or most vigorous kind, but sweet, true, and tender in its degree.

Dunfermline Press.—The poems abound in illustrations from a wide range of sources, as well as in the neat, short, and striking word-pictures which bespeak the author's care and accuracy, as well as the abundance of his literary information, both ancient and modern.

Border Advertiser.—We have not space to permit us to analyse with anything like justice the genius of our author. To say that the book is the production of genius is perhaps enough for our readers—especially in those days when genius is such a carce commodity.

Haddingtonshire Courier.—If the mission of the poet is to inculcate the principles of goodness and truth, and to cheer men in this world, then we must say that Mr Anderson has not come far short of this mission. His poetry has none of the drawing-room tones, or the tinge of the midnight lamp. It has the real ring of nature's poetry in it.

Hamilton Advertiser.—We cordially recommend the book itself to our readers. It will repay perusal, and is sure to afford much intellectual pleasure and enjoyment.

Dumfries-shire and Galloway Herald.—Many will be proud that the mine of poetry is still unexhausted within her (Dumfries) bounds, and the sons of labour should delight to honour one who has done so much to dignify their calling. They will find much in these poems to raise them in the scale of being.

Chicago Tribune.—There is a hearty earnestness about "Surfaceman's" poetry which at once engages the reader's attention, and keeps him spell-bound till he reaches the end of the poem.

www.ingramcontent.com/pod-product-compliance
Lightning Source LLC
Chambersburg PA
CBHW021938240426
43669CB00047B/461